CH

MYSTERIOUS PERSONS IN HISTORY

MYSTERIOUS PERSONS IN HISTORY

BAFFLING CASES OF UNSOLVED MYSTERIES

Fred Neff

℞ RUNESTONE PRESS • MINNEAPOLIS

Acknowledgments

All photos copyrighted to and reproduced with the permission of: UPI/Corbis-Bettmann, pp. 12, 43, 85; Corbis-Bettmann, p. 58; Archive Photos, pp. 69, 97, 103.

Cover photo/p. 31 courtesy of Archive Photos/Popperfoto.

Runestone Press
a division of Lerner Publications Company
241 First Avenue North
Minneapolis, MN 55401

Library of Congress Cataloging-in-Publication Data

Neff, Fred.
    Mysterious persons in history : baffling cases of unsolved mysteries / by Fred Neff.
      p.   cm.
    Includes bibliographical references.
    Summary: Discusses eight unsolved cases of mysterious death, from the nineteenth and early twentieth centuries, involving Napoleon Bonaparte, Sir Harry Oaks, the Black Dahlia, William Taylor, Lizzie Borden, Jack the Ripper, Dr. Sam Sheppard, and John Dillinger.
    ISBN 0–8225–3932–2 (alk. paper)
    1. History—Miscellanea—Juvenile literature. 2. Murderers—Biography—Juvenile literature. 3. Murder victims—Biography—Juvenile literature. [1. History—Miscellanea. 2. Murder—Case studies.] I. Title.
D21.3.N44 1997
364.15'23—dc21   96-51182

Manufactured in the United States of America
1 2 3 4 5 6 – JR – 02 01 00 99 98 97

This book is dedicated to Christa Neff, Theresa Freeman and Margaret McCoy, who unselfishly and enthusiastically gave their talent and time to this book from its inception to completion.

Contents

Introduction

The lives of the people in this book prove the truth of the old saying, truth is stranger than fiction. We all marvel at movie story lines, but few characters of the silver screen have lives that are more complex and intriguing than the fascinating people selected for inclusion in this book. Each of these people's lives is so controversial that it has taken on historical significance and presents an unsolved mystery that has remained of enduring interest over time. Through examining their lives the reader learns the history of the times they lived in and the puzzling questions surrounding these mysterious people.

The past acts as the roots of our lives. A study of the mysterious persons selected for this book gives the reader facts on historical figures, customs, and events. Many misconceptions may be exploded by such a study including the myth of the "good old days." Through the study of mysterious people of the past, we learn to better understand ourselves and the world we live in today. The reader can view the facts presented about these mysterious people and draw his or her own conclusion as to whether they were treated fairly during their lifetime and, still later, through historical accounts. The controversial nature of the people selected gives rise to questions of whether facts surrounding their lives have been destroyed, distorted or concealed by advocates for a particular cause in an attempt to impact events or to change historical records. Readers can look beyond this book to gather facts and draw their own unique answer to the mysteries surrounding the lives of these historical people. Trying to solve the mysteries surrounding these people should prove enjoyable and educational. The reader may act as a historical sleuth by carefully gathering facts, observing the evidence, making reasonable deductions from available information and then reasoning out the solution to the mystery.

1

Lizzie Borden

"Lizzie Borden took an axe, gave her mother forty whacks, when she saw what she had done, she gave her father forty-one." The rhyme about Lizzie Borden's callous attitude toward the killing of each of her parents has become a part of American folklore. The legend of Lizzie Borden has acted as the source for numerous stories about a mad axe murderess in stage plays, televisions shows, and movies. No depiction or derivation of the Borden murders can ever compare for macabre interest with the real story.

The world famous murder mystery began in Fall River, Massachusetts in August of 1892. Lizzie Borden lived at the time with her father Andrew Borden, stepmother Abbey Borden, and older sister Emma Borden. In the first week of August, both Mr. and Mrs. Borden came down with a mysterious sickness that went undiagnosed. On Thursday, August 4, 1892, Lizzie's uncle, John Morris, was a visitor who was staying with the Bordens. That morning, Abbey Borden came down to tell their maid, Bridgett Sullivan, how to prepare the breakfast. They were later joined by John Morris and Andrew Borden for breakfast. Lizzie did not come downstairs to eat breakfast with her parents, nor was her sister Emma present as she was away supposedly visiting friends in a nearby city. After the meal, Abbey Borden told the maid to wash the windows while she started to dust the home. Lizzie's uncle, John Morris, took a walk out of the home to do some visiting. Andrew Borden went to work outside of the home.

At about 10:45 in the morning, Bridgett Sullivan, the maid, heard the doorbell. When Bridgett went to answer it, she found that the door was locked and bolted tightly. This wasn't usually the way the door was positioned during the daytime. While unlocking the door she heard someone at the top of the stairs laughing. When the door was finally opened, Andrew Borden walked in and was greeted by his daughter, Lizzie, who had descended the stairs. She explained that his wife, Abbey, had earlier received a note from a sick person and gone out to help. Mr. Borden then decided to take a nap before the next meal. The maid also retired upstairs to her third floor bedroom to rest.

At about 11:00 A.M. a neighbor, Adelaide Churchill, observed Bridgett Sullivan rushing home from the doctor's house across the street. Mrs. Churchill approached Lizzie who was standing near the screen door of the Borden house to see if anything was wrong. She was to be the first person living outside the Borden home to be intro-

Lizzie Borden, 1892

duced to the horrors of that morning's work. It seems that the maid had gone to get the doctor because Lizzie's father, Andrew, had been killed. When Doctor Bowen arrived he found that the dead man had received repeated wounds to the skull caused by ten blows from an axe or hatchet. When Doctor Bowen left to send a telegram to Emma Borden, Mrs. Churchill asked Lizzie about her stepmother. Lizzie explained that she believed her mother had come back into the house. Bridgett Sullivan and Mrs. Churchill, in looking upstairs, confirmed that Mrs. Borden was in the house. Her body lay upstairs in the guest bedroom in a pool of blood having received nineteen blows, again from an axe or hatchet. It appeared as though Abbey Borden may have been working on the bedspread when she was caught off guard by the killer. That day police went in and out of the Borden home continually looking for clues to the killer. They found very little solid evidence to substantiate the story told in the later-created rhyme about Lizzie Borden.

At first Lizzie had the sympathy of many of her neighbors. She was known to be pious and civic-minded. She had been a Sunday school teacher and active in the community most of her adult life. Some people accepted the explanation that the murders had been performed by an enemy of Mr. Borden who took advantage of the gap in time when nobody was around, to kill him and his wife. A close relative of the Bordens indicated that there may have even been a money motive for the murders.

To some people, it seemed that Lizzie was not as upset over the murders as would be expected. They viewed her relatively calm demeanor after the murders as an obvious lack of concern for the loss of her father and stepmother. Her stoic acceptance of the situation seemed an acknowledgment of her guilt.

Emma Borden claimed the alibi of having been out of town visiting friends. There is no proof, however, that her alibi was ever officially corroborated. The Borden's house guest on the morning of the murder, John Morris, had an airtight alibi. His other relatives claimed to have been with him at the time of the murders. The Borden's maid, Bridgett Sullivan explained that on the morning of August 4, 1892, she was first outside cleaning the windows and then later in the morning she was upstairs on the third floor of the house far removed from the scene of the murders.

A coroner's inquest was held to determine the deaths of the Bordens. Lizzie Borden explained at the inquest that on the morning of the killings at least part of the time she was in the barn looking for some iron sinkers for a fishing line. She also related that she had been eating pears under a tree that morning. When questioned about her specific activities that morning, she gave contradictory explanations of events. Lizzie was asked where she had been when her father came back to the house on the morning of the killings. One time her answer was that she was on the stairs. At another time of the inquiry, she directly contradicted her own explanation and said she was in the kitchen at the time her father came back into the house that morning.

Suspicion soon centered on Lizzie Borden. She had no real alibi, just her own contradictory explanation of her actions. Lizzie's cool delivery of the events of the morning in question again made listeners wonder whether she cared about the death of her father and stepmother. She was not obviously as bereaved as people expected her to be with the death of her parents. After the inquest, it was claimed that Lizzie had been under the effect of morphine prescribed by her doctor to calm her down. This raises troubling questions. Was Lizzie Borden's calm demeanor a product of her guilt or simply the effect of a drug upon a bereaved person? Did Lizzie give contradictory explanations of her activities on the August 4, 1892, because she was being untruthful or under the cloud of a drug?

Authorities further doubted Lizzie because it was revealed that before the morning of the killing she had attempted to buy prussic acid to supposedly clean a coat. The druggist did not sell her the acid. The nagging question was presented as to why Lizzie Borden wanted to buy a poison like prussic acid in the hot summer to clean a coat to be worn in the winter? There was suspicion that the illness that her parents had experienced earlier in the week was not a product of the heat or ordinary upset stomachs, but of Lizzie's attempt to poison them. After failing to kill her parents by poison did Lizzie then resort to using a hatchet to accomplish her goal?

The police found several weapons in the Borden home that they believed could have killed the Bordens. One hatchet even supposedly had a broken handle. Its head was covered with ashes. Did someone attempt to wash off blood on the hatchet head and then disguise it with ashes?

The inquest itself remains controversial. Lizzie Borden's defense attorney had been barred from representing her at the hearing. She was not allowed the help of counsel during the inquiry. There is the serious question over

Lizzie's competency to testify at the inquest if she was under the effects of morphine. Does someone who appears calm on the surface necessarily feel the same way in their mind? Was Lizzie Borden's demeanor a product of morphine that had been given to her to calm her down, or an indication of her lack of remorse for the killings performed by her? Could her confusion as to the facts and contradictory statements be the product of a guilty mind or simply confusion brought on by the drugs?

It was the decision of the inquest at the end of the third day on August 11, 1892, that Lizzie Borden should be charged with the murders of her father and step-mother. A preliminary hearing was set for August 22, 1892. Did the prosecution have a real case against Lizzie Borden or was she a victim who was the easiest target for prosecution? After all, the police at the inquest did not have proof that they had found the actual murder weapon. The murder of Mr. Borden had taken place just before Mrs. Churchill greeted Lizzie. If the police did not have the actual murder weapon, then when could Lizzie Borden have found the time to conceal the instrument that delivered the deadly blows? There was no proof that Lizzie even left the house after the discovery of her father's body. If the police, after searching the house many times, could not find the murder weapon, was it not more consistent to believe that someone other than Lizzie had committed the murder and taken the weapon outside the home? To some people an even greater weakness in the prosecutor's case lay in the nature of Lizzie Borden herself as a potential suspect for the murder. In late nineteenth-century America a well-educated and respected person like Lizzie Borden was not thought to have been capable of the gory murder of her parents with a hatchet.

People who thought Lizzie could have committed the murders questioned if someone like her who was well-bred, would spend her time in a barn on a hot August morning looking for sinkers. There was the more serious question of why Lizzie would want to clean a warm seal-skin coat in the middle of the hot, humid summer. There were many questions about Lizzie's activities that would have to be considered to decide her probable guilt in murdering her parents.

Before a person in Massachusetts in 1892 could be sent to trial, it was necessary for a grand jury to inquire as to whether there were sufficient facts that would make it necessary for Lizzie Borden to have to go to a trial where her guilt or innocence on a murder charge would be determined. At the grand jury hearing evidence was brought out that Lizzie had burned a dress in front of her sister and a friend after her parents were murdered. Did Lizzie Borden destroy the bloodstained murder dress to cover up her crime? Based upon this and the other evidence that was presented to the grand jury, it was determined that it would be necessary for Lizzie Borden to go to trial in front of a jury to determine her guilt or innocence.

The actual trial for murder did not start until June 5, 1893. At that time Lizzie appeared in front of a three judge panel. She was represented by an illustrious team of lawyers including a former governor of her state, George Robinson.

The prosecution opened up the case by alleging Lizzie Borden was obviously guilty of the crime based on the fact that she was the only person who had a clear motive to kill her father and stepmother. The prosecutor pointed out that Lizzie had a desire for fine things. If she felt her future inheritance might be lost by a new will giving her father's wealth to his new wife, then Lizzie would have great motivation to kill her stepmother and father before the will was made. Further, the prosecution alleged that she was the only one of the immediate family that was in the home at the time of the murders. Her story of where she was at specific times on the morning of the murders left her credibility open to question. It was argued that if she didn't commit the murders, why did she burn a dress shortly after the murders? The prosecution even presented a hatchet with a broken handle as the murder weapon.

The testimony of witnesses at the trial did not, however, fully support the prosecution's case. For example, the prosecution introduced a witness to show that someone would have been able to clearly see Lizzie's stepmother's dead body if he or she was standing on the steps, the implication being that Lizzie knew of her stepmother's death long before Mrs. Borden's body was found. The prosecution gave the impression that Lizzie had kept quiet about Abbey Borden's fate because she was the killer. The witness for the prosecution, however, on cross examination stated that when taking photographs after the murder it was found that a body positioned in a similar manner to the way Mrs. Borden's body was after the murder could not be seen unless the viewer was at the top of the stairs in a particular position. Further, the prosecution could not prove through witnesses that the dress that Lizzie Borden burned was the same one that she was wearing on the morning of the murders. As the case developed, it appeared as though the prosecution had overstated their case.

Lizzie's defense team was effectively able to get the judges to strike out the testimony of the inquest witness about the prussic acid that Lizzie allegedly attempted to buy. This information the prosecution believed could have been quite telling in that it could have indicated that Lizzie had an intent to commit murder before the day in question by her attempt to purchase prussic acid. It could also have opened the door to further consideration that the sickness that her parents experienced at a time before the day of the murders was caused by poison introduced by Lizzie. The defense also was able to get the judges to exclude Lizzie's inquest testimony which had so dangerously shown her contradicting herself.

The defense struck possibly its greatest blow to the prosecution's case by destroying the argument that the broken-handled hatchet was the murder weapon. It was shown that the hatchet could not be proven to be the murder weapon since it did not have blood stains, as expected, on it. Even the prosecution's argument that Lizzie could not have been in the barn because the dust in it was undisturbed was weakened by witnesses that claimed to have been in the barn right after the murder. If the investigators did not find their footprints in the dust, then the investigators had not properly reviewed the floor. Otherwise, they would have found that someone had actually been in the barn before their search. Defense witnesses even described people of unknown identity that were around the Borden house at the time of the murders. This type of evidence created a question as to an unknown killer or Mr. X. Could there have been a person outside the family that had actually performed the murders? The question as to the unknown assailant loomed increasingly larger as the prosecution's case against Lizzie fell apart.

It was necessary for the prosecution to prove that Lizzie Borden was guilty beyond a reasonable doubt. Lizzie's quiet, gentle demeanor coupled with the effectiveness of her attorney's defense cut through the strong cord of evidence against her. In its closing argument the defense did not underplay that the double murder was heinous. Instead, Lizzie's attorney asserted that only a monster could perform such a crime. Could Lizzie Borden, a former Sunday School teacher, be a monster who would brutally kill her parents with a hatchet?

One of the judges in summing up the case was careful to urge the jury to ignore what they had read in the press and to seek the truth. There was, in essence, the point of Lizzie's fine character. The judges' comments even rationalized some of the defendant's behavior. After the judges' summaries, the jury retired to make a consideration. Did Lizzie Borden, the potential heir to a $500,000 estate which could have been lost by a change of will, kill her parents to secure her inheritance? Was the prosecution pursuing Lizzie Borden because she was the easiest target? Did the circumstantial evidence that she was in the house at the time of the murders and could not give a consistent story show that she was the murderess? Could a gentle woman of the Victorian Era commit such a heinous crime as a double hatchet murder simply to secure her inheritance?

Many arguments took place during the trial over Lizzie Borden's guilt or innocence, but it would be the jury, based upon the evidence presented, who would ultimately decide her fate. They returned in just over an hour to bring in a verdict. The jury foreman announced the verdict of not guilty. Lizzie Borden sank into her chair as the courtroom went wild with cheers.

After the trial, Lizzie Borden retired to her family's home with her sister, Emma. Up to that time Emma was the sole beneficiary and responsible for the inherited estate from her father. After the trial, Lizzie was able to share in the inheritance. Emma and Lizzie bought a large home in an exclusive part of her town. The two drifted apart and ended up living in separate places.

Within three years after being acquitted of the murders, Lizzie became involved in a new controversy. This time she was accused of stealing two porcelain paintings from an art gallery. She was led to believe that there would be no prosecution if she would only admit to committing the murders. After some resistance it was said that Lizzie typed a note that in essence stated that under duress she was admitting the act of August 4, 1892. Ever afterwards, people who were interested in the Borden case, have argued over whether Lizzie's alleged confession was true or made under duress.

If Lizzie Borden did not commit the murders then who did? Could the murders have been done by the maid, Bridgett Sullivan? If Bridgett committed the murders what was her motive for doing so? Could the pressure of having to cook and clean the windows on a hot day when she was ill been enough to cause Bridgett to kill her employer? Could Lizzie Borden's sister Emma have committed the murders? Could it have been an act of protection for both her own and Lizzie's financial welfare that

21

prompted her to commit the murders? Was the alibi that Emma was visiting a friend in a nearby town valid? Could Emma have visited the friend, but sneaked away for long enough to have committed the acts of murder? Was the order of the murders (Mrs. Borden was killed first and then Lizzie's father) proof that the murder was well thought out by a member of the family? By killing the mother first, the killer made sure that Mrs. Borden's relatives would not inherit any of Mr. Borden's estate. Could Emma have planned the murders, so she would end up in charge of the estate and not suspect because she was out of town at the time of the murders?

There even is the story that in the later years of Emma Borden's life she moved to a small town in New Hampshire. In the house where she lived, she allegedly had built a special panel that illuminated the downstairs, and a secret closet where an axe was stored. Does the story of Emma's last place of residence indicate she was the real murderess who expected to someday be caught? Could it be that Lizzie committed the killings in a conspiracy with her sister Emma? The sisters could have developed a plan where Lizzie would make sure that the door was locked from the inside so no one would interfere while the first murder was being committed. Could an outsider have committed the murders? Many questions still arise out of the incredible tale of the Borden murders of 1892. Will anyone ever know if Lizzie Borden committed the crime? Possibly not, but history has a way of keeping alive a story that is just too good to kill.

2

Jack the Ripper

A beautiful young woman dressed in Victorian finery walks along the streets of London at night and is suddenly approached by a tall man with a black flowing cape and floppy felt hat with the brim turned down. He quickly puts one hand over her mouth while his other hand uses a knife to slash her throat with surgical precision. She falls to the ground and he briskly moves away into the shadows. This scene has been replayed in scores of stage productions and movies. It is based on the killings in 1888 in Victorian England that capture anew each succeeding generation in their web of circumstance and mystery.

How historically accurate is the stereotype of Jack the Ripper as a tall mysterious stranger dressed in black who slashes beautiful women's throats and then disappears? In order to understand the Ripper, one must first understand the city of London, England, in 1888. Late twentieth century descriptions of Victorian England often emphasize the earlier era's glory, genteel charm, and freedom from the pressures of modern society. People are reminded of the power and majesty of Victorian England by the old saying, "The sun never sets on the British Empire." While Victorian England was basking in its world power, thousands of immigrants from all over Europe poured into the largest city in that country in order to be able to gain opportunities that would uplift their lives. They often ended up in areas of London such as Whitechapel, where they lived in poverty and squalor. Jack the Ripper frequented this poverty-stricken area and not the fashionable residential areas of London. His victims were not attractive young women of fashion, but the downtrodden who worked at prostitution to provide for necessities. The folklore of Jack the Ripper tells that he murdered five women from August 31, 1888, to November 9, 1888, and then mysteriously disappeared into history. Although this presents a tantalizing enigma, it may be inaccurate.

Murder was not an uncommon event in London in 1888. Women who worked as prostitutes were highly vulnerable to being victims of the most serious of all crimes. Even before August 31, 1888, which was the date of the killing of the first of the five traditionally accepted victims of Jack the Ripper, prostitutes were frequently murdered in London. Earlier murder victims in 1888 are not generally accepted as Ripper victims, because their wounds did not give the impression that the killer was trying to dissect their body with surgical precision. For example, earlier in August of 1888 a prostitute, Martha Tabram, alias Martha Turner, was stabbed 39 times with a weapon. These wounds resembled what might have been made by a bayonet. The suspect seemed possibly to be a soldier or guard. The Martha Turner murder remains unsolved and controversial. Did Jack the Ripper start with simple stabbing attacks and graduate to more severe acts of mutilation? Couldn't Martha Turner have been an early victim of Jack the Ripper?

In the early morning of August 31, 1888, in London, England, a man walking along Bucks Row observed a bundle lying in the street. As he approached it, he observed that the bundle was the body of a woman who was apparently drunk. The woman's head lay in the gutter with her body across the entrance to an old stable yard. The police and a physician were called to the scene. After finding that the woman was dead, her body was transferred to a morgue. A policeman at the morgue made a more careful inspection of the woman's body than had been performed by the people who found it. He discovered the extent of the brutalization of the victim. The body of the mysterious woman had been ripped open from the throat to the stomach. It was later discovered that her name was Mary Ann Nichols. She was commonly known by the name of Polly Nichols. The victim was not the glamorous, carefree young beauty that is depicted in some movies, but instead a poor forty-two-year-old woman, who worked to support her desire for alcohol. Many Ripperologists believe that Polly Nichols was the first of the victims because of the grotesque wounds found on her dead body. This murder set the stage for what was to come in the following weeks. What may have been even more strange than the damage inflicted on the victim's body was the fact that her murderer was able to escape from one of the earth's most concentrated areas of people, without any witnesses observing him. At the time of Polly Nichols's murder, there was a policeman on patrol near the area where her body was found. At the same time, people were getting up out of bed in order to go to work, while others were returning home. This showed the skill or the phenomenal luck of the man later called Jack the Ripper.

In the early hours of Saturday, September 8, Annie Chapman, a prostitute who frequented the area of London called Whitechapel, was turned away from a lodging house because she could not pay the bill for a bed. Later that day she was found in the corner of a nearby yard with her windpipe severed. Near her body was found an envelope with the corner torn off. Close by Annie Chapman's feet were laid out two brass rings, a few pennies, and some farthings. Did Annie Chapman's killer take the coins from her and symbolically place them by her or were they a ritualistic payment by him out of his own money? If the pennies and farthings at Annie Chapman's feet were taken from her by the killer, then why didn't she use them earlier to pay for the rooming house?

Once again it was not until the body of Annie Chapman had been moved to the mortuary that a doctor discovered the extent of her injuries, which were even more severe than the earlier victim, Mary Ann Nichols. There were numerous stabs and cuts on the victim. Certain internal organs had been taken out of the body by the murderer. In a curious repetition of the earlier mutilation of Mary Ann Nichols, the two front teeth of Annie Chapman had been removed by the killer. Dr. Phillips, who had examined the body of Annie Chapman, expressed the opinion at her inquest that the murderer must have had knowledge of the human body and medical skill, otherwise he could not have so quickly and efficiently performed the terrible deed.

The worst was yet to come, for on September 30, 1888, on Berner Street at about 1:00 A.M., a cartman, Mr. Delmschutz, was surprised when the pony that was pulling the cart that he drove seemed frightened and reluctant to move. He dismounted the cart to see just what was keeping his pony from proceeding. To his surprise the body of a woman, Elizabeth Stride, was lying against the wall. He promptly went to get help. A later medical exam of the body revealed that the dead woman's throat was slit. From observations of the body and witnesses in the area of Berner Street that night, it was gathered that Ms. Stride must have been killed shortly before she was found by the cartman. Her body did not, however, show the type of mutilation observed in the earlier murders. Two explanations that have been proposed to explain the lack of mutilation are that either Ms. Stride was not killed by the Ripper or the murderer was interrupted before he could finish the job. There was speculation that when Mr. Delmschutz found the body, the killer may still have been nearby. Could the murderer have been waiting around the corner a few feet behind him with knife in hand? The Ripper may have gone around the cart and slipped away from the murder scene after Mr. Delmschutz went to get help.

At about the same time as the murderer was escaping from the scene of the crime near Berner Street, a prostitute by the name of Katherine Eddowes was being let out of jail where she had been held for drunkenness for the preceding five hours. Little did she know that leaving jail was not going to liberate her, but instead lead to her death. Unfortunately, Ms. Eddowes was to meet the murderer who later became widely known as Jack the Ripper. A very short time after Ms. Eddowes left the jail a policeman found her dead body which had been stabbed repeatedly. Once again internal organs had been taken out of the body of the murdered woman. The killer again left evidence. A fragment that was torn away from an apron had been used to wipe off blood. The city police found a sink nearby where it appeared the murderer had washed his hands. The murderer may have been frightened away before he had an opportunity to finish washing his hands. He may have continued to wipe off his hands as he moved away from the spot, because a piece of the blood-stained apron was found a short distance from the scene of the murder.

The day after the double murder, the central news agency received a letter in red ink signed Jack the Ripper. This was the second letter that they had received bearing this signature. Before the double murder, they had received another written communication promising that there would be some more work in the near future and that the Ripper, as he called himself, would be clipping off his victims' ears and sending them to the police. The first letter, however, had been thought to be a hoax, but the two murders of September 30, 1888, changed their impressions of it. The two letters were now taken seriously since there had been an attempt to cut off the ear of the victim on Berner Street and the second letter that they received apologized for the fact that no ear had been sent. It explained that the reason was because there had been an interruption. If the murder of Annie Chapman had brought public attention to the terrible acts perpetrated upon prostitutes that fall in London, it was nothing to the hysteria that swept England when the press revealed the double murder of September 30, 1888. Some citizens even demanded that the Commissioner of Police, Charles Warren, resign since he was not able to stop the terrible mutilations and murders. There were many theories as to the identity of the killer and even suggestions as to how to catch him.

Investigations into the possible identity of the victims revealed that the woman killed at Berner Street was Elizabeth Stride. She had taken to extensive drinking of alcohol and prostitution after undergoing an emotional upheaval in her life. The other victim, Katherine Eddowes, was at first wrongly identified as an Irish woman named Mary Ann Kelly. Later it was established that her true name was Katherine Eddowes. She was a woman of forty-five years of age who, like the earlier victims before her, had been caught in poverty and prostitution.

It was interesting that the next victim turned out to be an attractive young prostitute by the name of Mary Kelly. Could the Ripper also have been confused about Katherine Eddowes's identity and killed her thinking she was Mary Kelly? A witness may have observed the Ripper walk off with Mary Kelly shortly before her death. He was described as a short, heavyset man with a curling mustache, who was carrying some type of parcel. Later, about 3:10 A.M. of November 9, 1888, a neighbor of Mary Kelly heard her cry "murder." There then was silence during which it is believed that Jack the Ripper dissected the body of his victim. Later the police were to find in Mary's apartment the remnants of what they believed to be burnt clothing in the grate of the fireplace. Many questions come to mind over the death scene of Mary Kelly. Did the killer burn the clothing to hide incriminating evidence or to create added heat to make it warmer in the room while he performed the macabre work? Whose clothing was actually burned? After the extensive dissection of the body there must have been a tremendous amount of blood all over the killer. Why wasn't he noticed walking through the streets of London? If he destroyed his own clothing, then what kind of clothing did he wear when he left Mary Kelly's apartment?

Some people have pointed out that the answers to these questions may be in the records of the police, a prison, a doctor's files, a mental institution or even a diary. This is nothing more than speculation, since the records that are available have yet to answer all the questions that have come out of the killings.

Modern day Ripperologists have differences of opinion as to the murderer's motivation. Some people think that the Ripper was a mad killer, who possibly hated prostitutes because of something that took place in his past. Other people believe that he was a sadistic killer who took pleasure in inflicting pain and drawing blood from his victims. Some students of the killings even believe he was a social reformer who was trying to draw attention to the terrible conditions that people experience in the ghetto areas of London.

Investigators who believe Jack the Ripper showed surgical skills have often believed he was a doctor. A midwife or nurse could also have performed certain medical procedures. Some people have even argued that the Ripper could have been a butcher. It seems that once a theory on the personality and motivation of the Ripper

A newspaper clipping showing Katherine Eddowes (left) and a man seen with her shortly before her murder. Police suspected this man of being Jack the Ripper.

developed the next step has been to look for an actual suspect with characteristics that dovetail with the theory. None of the popular suspects meet all necessary criteria to prove he was the killer beyond a reasonable doubt. Generally, a suspect should have a motive to kill, have had an opportunity to commit the crime, and lack an alibi. There should also be sufficient evidence to indicate the suspect actually committed the crime.

One theory is that the Ripper was a Dr. Stanley, who was tremendously attached to an only son. When his son died after contacting a type of venereal disease from a prostitute, Mary Kelly, Dr. Stanley devoted his life to a search for that woman. He ended up murdering any prostitute that had been questioned in an effort to find Mary Kelly. Once he found and killed her the terrible murder spree of the Ripper ended. Dr. Stanley allegedly ended his life by making a confession in Buenos Aires. To this day, however, there is some question as to whether there was a Dr. Stanley.

The well-known criminal, George Chapman, has sometimes been identified as the Ripper. It has been argued that he was really a Polish immigrant by the name of Severin Klossowski, who worked as a barber in Whitechapel during the Ripper murders. Later, after the Mary Kelly murder in 1888, Chapman traveled to the United States and later returned to England in 1892. He eventually was found to have murdered three women for no clear motive during the ten years from 1892 to 1902. Chapman was executed in 1903. One of the chief investigators in the Ripper murders, an Inspector Abberline, indicated he believed George Chapman was the real Jack the Ripper. In support of the theory that George Chapman, alias Severin

Klossowski, was the real killer is that similar types of Ripper murders allegedly took place in Jersey City in the United States while he was living there in 1890. It is, however, hard to accept that a killer like George Chapman would change his method of committing murder. Why would he start out committing vicious killings with a knife and then go to the passive method of using poison to end his victims' lives? There also seems to be a difference in the type of relationship that George Chapman and Jack the Ripper had with their victims. The Ripper chose as his victims, prostitutes, who were most likely encountered in the street while Chapman instead chose as victims women whom he knew very well and lived with for a while.

It has been claimed that Rasputin, the famous Russian monk who was a consultant used by Russian royalty during World War I, left a document which set out the identity of Jack the Ripper. He was supposedly an insane Russian who had been sent to England by the Czar's police to embarrass the English police. The Russian immigrant was a barber and surgeon by the name of Pedachenko. A Russian secret police gazette supposedly reported the death of Pedachenko in a Russian mental home. That same paper allegedly explained that he had killed five women in the West End of London in 1888. There is, however, a lack of clear proof of the existence of this particular issue of the gazette. Pedachenko has been described as a short, broad-shouldered man with a large mustache who was well dressed. This would match up in some ways with the description by the witness who observed the person walking away with Mary Kelly. It has been said that Pedachenko may have had two helpers to assist him in committing the murders. Some people have even speculated that Pedachenko may have been the same person as George Chapman. There is not strong documentation that Pedachenko actually lived in London at the time of the Whitechapel murders. Other students of the Jack the Ripper legend claim that Pedachenko is nothing more than a literary creation, who was developed to give an interesting background and identity for the Ripper. Possibly Pedachenko fulfills the commonly accepted stereotype of the Ripper being both a madman and a doctor.

A young lawyer, Montague John Druitt, who had a history of mental illness and instability, was another person accused of being Jack the Ripper. Some people believe that he ended up living near the area of the murders. They argue he knew the neighborhood where the murders occurred so well that he could commit the terrible deeds and avoid being caught. The argument that Montague John Druitt was the Ripper is allegedly supported by the claim that he was mentally ill, had exposure to medical knowledge, and was found dead a month after the Mary Kelly murder. His death would explain why no more was heard from Jack the Ripper after November 9, 1888. Still there are nagging questions about M. J. Druitt being Jack the Ripper. Just because someone is mentally ill, it does not mean that he would be dangerous to others. There is insufficient data available on Druitt's background to show that he took out his hostility in a manner that would indicate he was the Ripper. If the murderer showed the surgical skill of a doctor, could he have gained it just from being exposed to people who practiced medicine? Although Druitt may have had relatives who were doctors, it does not necessarily mean that he would have had the skill to perform the murders like a skilled surgeon.

What is intriguing about Druitt is the way he died. It seems that he was drowned and that rocks were found inside his coat pockets. Some people believe that Druitt committed suicide because he wanted to end his horrible existence and avoid the possibility that he would end up in a mental institution. There still remains the question of why Druitt, who was supposedly a strong swimmer, would choose drowning as a way to commit suicide? Why would stones be put in the pockets of Druitt's coat when he could have ended his life in a simpler manner? Could the stones in his pocket instead show that Druitt was the victim of murder? The many unanswered questions surrounding M. J. Druitt seriously weaken the likelihood he was the Ripper.

James Maybrick, a prominent merchant from Liverpool who died of arsenic poisoning in the year after the Ripper murders, is another candidate. Supporters of Maybrick as the Ripper cite the existence of a diary allegedly prepared by Maybrick that shows he may have been so greatly affected by arsenic and his wife's suspected adultery that he became mentally ill and took out his rage on prostitutes. Further, support for Maybrick as the Ripper has arguably come from a gold watch found in Liverpool with scratches that supposedly show the signature of J. Maybrick with the further wording of, "I am Jack the Ripper." The diary and watch have been challenged as a hoax. Although Maybrick may be a candidate, a substantial part of the strength of his claim remains in the highly controversial evidence of the diary and watch.

One of the more publicized candidates for the title of

Jack the Ripper was the Duke of Clarence, who would have been in line to become the King of England. The theory has been that the Duke showed a very erratic mental state. It has been argued he took to murdering prostitutes and that the English government covered it up. There are, however, gaps and flaws in this theory. It seems that at critical times when the murders took place the Duke may have been out of London. The Duke could have sneaked back into town, but there was some evidence that this was not the case. Another thing that weakens the case for the Duke of Clarence as a potential killer, is the fact that there is very little in his background to show he was capable of the type of violence committed by the murderer of the prostitutes in Whitechapel. Besides, if the Ripper was a doctor, there has been no evidence that the Duke of Clarence had any special medical skill. Possibly, the only clear thing that would indicate that the Duke of Clarence could have been related to the crimes, was that he may have spent time in recreational activities near the area of the murders. This alone, however, does not indicate that he was the killer. In the Victorian Era it was not uncommon for even royalty to visit night spots and places of recreation near the part of the city where the victims were found. If just visiting these recreation spots makes someone a candidate for the Ripper, then a great many more aristocrats and people of wealth would be suspect.

In line with the idea that Jack the Ripper was a medical person and possibly assisted by accomplices is a fascinating theory of conspiracy. Supposedly, the famous artist, Walter Sickert, was a tutor to the Duke of Clarence. It was during this time the Duke of Clarence allegedly became familiar with a young woman who was living in the east end of London. He secretly married her, which presented a great complication for the monarchy since she was not of royal blood. If this became open knowledge, it could cause a public uproar. Later, she had a child by the Duke which made the whole matter extremely dangerous since it could affect the succession to the throne of England. It could open up the possibility that a child of a non-royal mother could succeed to the crown.

In order to minimize the potential danger in the situation, the Duke and his wife were separated by government agents. Later she was put into a mental institution while the Duke was kept under close scrutiny. The famous Dr. William Gull, who acted as a physician to the royal family, was put in charge of hushing up witnesses to the situation. He allegedly chose a permanent way to end the gossip. Dr. Gull, with the help of Walter Sickert and the coachman who had brought the Duke of Clarence on earlier trips down to Whitechapel, set about a course to end the possible threat by killing the prostitutes, who had knowledge of the Duke's marriage. Sickert had been chosen because he knew the prostitutes and could lure them into the trap of the executioner, Dr. William Gull. This might explain why the prostitutes would go along with a man even though there was clearly fear in the air after the Mary Ann Nichols murder. If there were three men involved in the conspiracy, it could also explain why there have been different descriptions of the men who were seen near the area of the murders.

One of the key questions that has been raised in the Jack the Ripper murders has been why there was so little blood found near the area of the murders. Some people argue that the blood was washed away with water by the police. Other students of the Ripper have made the point that the blood was absorbed by the victims' clothing. Still other Ripperologists claim it was the way that the cuts were made that eliminated a lot of potential blood. One other possible solution is that a victim was not killed at the place where her body was found. A victim could have been lured into a coach where she was then murdered. Later the prostitute's body was dropped off at the place where the victim was discovered. If the major part of the bleeding took place inside the coach it could explain why there was not much blood found near the place where the victim was found. Supposedly, the three men in the conspiracy theory worked together to get a prostitute into the coach where she was murdered in a surgical manner by Dr. Gull. The murder spree ended when the last prostitute with knowledge of the royal scandal was killed. Some people even believe that after the murders concluded with Mary Kelly on November 9, 1888, Dr. Gull was institutionalized for mental illness. The story explains that Dr. William Gull actually lived far beyond the date that is commonly given for his death. A false funeral was held for him and an empty casket was buried in his grave. This was to allow him to keep his excellent reputation intact. He was institutionalized for his mental illness while the public believed that he had been buried after a distinguished career.

This theory has not settled once and for all the controversy over the identity of Jack the Ripper, but instead brought forth new challenges to be answered. What actual proof of the marriage of the Duke of Clarence to the young lady from the Whitechapel area actually is in existence? Were distinguished and respected people like Walter Sickert and Dr. William Gull capable of the unsavory and ritualistic acts of murder assigned to the Jack the Ripper character?

It has always been far easier for some people to believe that Jack the Ripper was a violent brute with very little education. They find it hard to accept that a professional person could have committed the brutal acts of murder in the fall of 1888 in the Whitechapel area. This is in spite of the fact that history has shown that killers come from all walks of life and both sexes. In recognition of this reality still another theory has been proposed. The person who took the lives of the London prostitutes in 1888 may have been a Jill the Ripper. Could the Ripper have been a midwife who murdered prostitutes? If the Ripper was a woman, in a medical occupation, she could have easily approached the prostitutes without them expecting harm. It may also explain why the killer was not noticed as she left the areas of the crime. Couldn't a woman have committed the brutal acts that have been credited to the Ripper character?

The murderer could even have been a policeman. No one would expect a policeman to commit such heinous crimes, nor would there be anything unusual about seeing a law enforcement officer in the area of the murders. Possibly the policeman had some reason for hating the prostitutes who were killed or needed to permanently stop them from revealing something that they knew was happening in the area. Although the theory of a corrupt and maniacal policeman seems possible, there is no evidence that any such officer ever participated in the Ripper murders.

What is clear is that although more than 100 years have passed since the Jack the Ripper murders, interest in the subject has not abated. The controversy over them appears to be a permanent part of the folklore of criminology that will remain fertile ground for further thrillers in book, play, and movie form in the future.

3

Sir Harry Oaks

A murder in the circles of the privileged and wealthy is always a matter of interest to the public. Very few killings, however, have caught the public's attention as much as that of Sir Harry Oaks, who was one of the wealthier people in the world when he died in 1943. The impact of the announcement of his death was so large, that it temporarily absorbed valuable space that would normally be covered by the daily news of the events of World War II. Harry Oaks's death is more than just a celebrity murder case, it is one of the more fascinating puzzles in the annals of crime.

To understand the Oaks murder case it is necessary to look back at the victim's life. Sir Harry Oaks was born in the state of Maine in the United States. Although his family was not wealthy, they did provide for an excellent education for young Harry. He began to attend medical school, but found that it was not to his liking. Harry wanted to become wealthy, but did not want to do it, he claimed, by taking advantage of other people. His great love was the outdoors with a special interest in trees. One day he hit upon the idea of finding his wealth in the earth itself. This idea germinated into an odyssey in search of gold that took him to Alaska, Russia, Australia, and Canada. Throughout twenty years of searching he remained unsuccessful. Harry Oaks was known to be one of the harder workers among the international goldmining community. He always persistently pursued his search for the elusive treasure. Finally, he hit upon one of the larger gold strikes in history in Canada. Once the find was made, he did not find life easy. Certain business groups tried to latch on and make claims to the development of Harry's gold interest. They did not find him an easy mark. Harry Oaks fought his way through the courts until he finally secured his legal rights to the mines and their utilization. Once this was accomplished, he set about the course of developing his mineral interests.

During the 1920s, Harry Oaks became one of the great Canadian entrepreneurs. Even his wealth did not give him the power and respectability he sought. When Canada heavily taxed Harry without giving him a feeling of being a valued citizen, he moved to the Bahama Islands off the southern part of the United States. Once in the Bahamas, Harry Oaks helped develop the beautiful islands to make them a better place for the inhabitants. He became one of the more important philanthropists in the Bahamas. Harry built an airfield, donated money to contribute to the building of a hospital, developed jobs

Sir Harry Oaks

for the inhabitants, and performed other acts of charity. In the late 1930s the English monarchy knighted Harry Oaks for his great efforts. Finally, Harry had found a measure of respectability. He developed a devoted interest in his new home in the Bahamas. Harry protectively and lovingly looked after the land. He was often seen working in the fields. New challenges, however, faced Harry. Although he had been able to pull from the earth one of its great treasures, fight and win legal battles, and even get the respectability of being knighted, he faced a challenge from business interests that wanted to commercialize his island paradise.

The Bahamas had long been a beautiful place for the wealthy to live. There were inhabitants of the islands, however, who felt that the land was being underutilized and should be used for an international resort area. Harry Oaks resisted the idea of his paradise becoming a resort capital that brought people in to gamble. He saw this kind of encroachment into his world as a direct threat. Although his wealth gave him great power, there were other people in the Bahamas who had the strength and respectability to influence the future of the islands. The former King of England, then known as the Duke of Windsor, was in 1942 the governor of the Bahamas. Although officially he appeared neutral on the issue of the use of the Bahamas after the war as a resort area, it appeared to many that he might be interested in such a development. He outwardly had respect for Harry Oaks, but had monetary needs at the time which made him open to looking for ways to add to his own financial power.

Another powerful force in the Bahamas was a man by the name of Harold Christie. He had formerly been involved in rum running and other questionable activities. He had, however, through intelligence and the strength of his efforts, become an influential real estate developer in the Bahamas. Mr. Christie, however, had connections with other groups and was one of the leading forces in moving towards bringing gambling into the Bahamas. He traveled in the same select circle as Harry Oaks and the Duke of Windsor. Many Bahamians looked at him as a person that they could go to, to help them with their economic difficulties.

Outside gambling interests that had long been active in Florida and Cuba started to bring pressure to bear in the early 1940s to have gambling legalized in the Bahamas. They could foresee that after World War II ended there would be a tremendous interest in additional resorts in the western hemisphere. There was a desire to open up gambling places in a safe haven, such as the Bahamas, that would be free from the potential political turmoil that was always under the surface in Cuba. This group may have tried to work through people like Harold Christie in order to get respectable power sources in the Bahamas to work with them on their plan. The largest group of people, however, which was gaining increasing power over the fate of the island, was the indigenous natives of the Bahamas. In the years that preceded the Second World War, the people who lived in the Bahamas appeared to play a very minor role in the development of the island. In the 1940s there became an increasing awareness on the part of the people of the Bahamas that they should take an active part in their own future, rather than leave it to a small group of the privileged.

Harry Oaks had exposure to each of the basic power

groups and many have questioned to what extent any of the groups either individually or in combination contributed to his death. It has been hard to show that any one of the major groups clearly had enough animosity toward Harry Oaks to actively play a part in his death. There was one individual, however, who was not a member of one of the groups who was pointed to as possibly having a motive for Harry's death. This person was Harry's own son-in-law, Fred Marigny. He had come to the Bahama Islands only recently from the United States. He claimed a noble title and was known to be one of the international playboy set. Marigny had been married before coming to the islands and did not demonstrate a serious desire to develop a business until he was in his thirties. Some people believe that he may have come to the Bahamas to avoid his ex-wife and to find a new source to tap into for money. When Marigny met Harry Oaks's daughter, Nancy, it was the start of a liaison that would become a great source of gossip in the Bahamas and anguish to the Oaks family.

Nancy was only a teenager when she fell under the influence of the wealthy and sophisticated Mr. Marigny. After she turned eighteen years old, Marigny traveled to New York where she was attending school and married her. When Harry Oaks learned that his daughter had married the older man without even getting his permission, a controversy arose that some people believed led to Harry's own demise. Although Harry and his wife tried to break up the couple, they were unsuccessful. On July 7, 1943, the Marignys were apart, not through anything that Harry Oaks had done, but simply because his wife had gone for a visit to the United States. While his wife was away, Marigny spent the evening in the company of a friend and a fellow countryman from Mauritius, the Marquis Georges de Visdelou-Guimbeau, along with two married women who had husbands that were in the Royal Air Force.

On the same evening Harry Oaks's wife was out of the country. He spent his evening with Harold Christie and two other friends. After the party broke up for the evening, Christie stayed the night at the Oaks's home as a guest. There seems to be a great deal of speculation and argument over the events that followed the hour when Harry Oaks and Harold Christie parted to go to their respective bedrooms. Mr. Christie maintained that he retired to his room and after awakening the next morning went to Sir Harry Oaks's room to bid him good morning. He found Harry's body laying on his bed burned in several places. The fire was still smoldering. There was fine soot lying about the room. To get help, Christie called the doctor and the police. A later examination of the room revealed that Harry Oaks was dead. He had apparently received an attack to his head by a blunt weapon that had caused a serious fracture. There were indications that he had a brain hemorrhage and had been in shock. The death room scene was unusual, for Harry's body showed indications of both being bludgeoned and burned. There were even feathers around the room that gave rise to speculation that they were left as a voodoo mark of death.

When Sir Harry Oaks's death was announced, the whole island was shocked. The Duke of Windsor, who was acting governor, decided to take over direct control of the case. He called the United States and arranged to have two policemen from Miami, Florida, come to the island to investigate. His act remains open to question, since the Bahamas were not a part of the United States. Some people thought that he should have called Scotland Yard to arrange to have experts flown in. If not Scotland Yard, some questioned, then why not the FBI, which had some of the leading experts in the world on forensic and criminal investigations?

After the Miami police arrived, they set about gathering fingerprint evidence from the scene of the crime. Officer Barker later claimed to have found a fingerprint of Fred Marigny's little finger on a screen near Sir Harry Oaks's bed. He also found that certain hair on Marigny's body looked to be scorched. The claim was that hair on his hand, beard, and forearm showed that they had been subjected recently to great heat. The other Miami policeman, Melchen, asserted that the smudge marks in the hall showed that Sir Harry Oaks had gone into the hall with his pajamas on fire and was forced back into his room and bed that was on fire. Melchen even claimed that Marigny told him that Sir Harry hated Marigny because he had married Nancy Oaks. Fred Marigny allegedly went on to state that he in turn hated Sir Harry Oaks because he was in essence a fool who was not reasonable.

Within a short time of the beginning of the investigation by the Miami police, they concluded that Fred Marigny was the lone killer of Sir Harry Oaks. The basis of their case was the fingerprint, scorched hair, and motivation to kill Harry Oaks. They reasoned that Marigny hated Sir Harry Oaks and had decided to do him in with the idea in mind that he would then have access to the wealth of the great man without having to deal with him. Interestingly, a colonel who was in charge of the Nassau police was transferred to another island before the trial took place.

On October 18, 1943, the trial of Fred Marigny began before Sir Oscar Daly, who was Chief Justice of the Bahamas. The Attorney General, the Honorable Eric Hallinan, led for the Crown, with one of Nassau's leading attorneys, the Honorable Alfred Adderley, to assist with the prosecution. The defense was led by Godfrey Higgs with the skilled assistance of Ernest Callender.

First it appeared that the sentiment in the courtroom was that Fred Marigny was an outsider and obviously open to committing the heinous crime of murder. The prosecution's reconstruction of the events that led to Harry's death, however, seemed questionable given the evidence that came out at trial. For example, Captain Melchen had claimed that Sir Harry Oaks had tottered into the hall and ended up leaning against the wall, but was forced back into the room. The medical evidence, however, seemed to show that Sir Harry had not necessarily been out of his bed. The Miami policeman did not give affirmative evidence that showed that he had done a thorough analysis of what material was actually used to start the fire in the bedroom. In fact, no adequate measurements had even been made of the hand marks on the walls of Sir Harry Oaks's room.

The sloppiness of the police investigation continued to show up in the prosecution's presentation. A bloodstained towel was allegedly found on Sir Harry Oaks's bed. In Harold Christie's room a towel with bloodstains was also discovered. No adequate explanation was given by the prosecution to explain why the bloodstains had been on the towel found in Christie's bedroom. The impression was given that the real estate developer may have found Sir Harry's body and poured water in his mouth. He also may have wet a towel to wipe off Sir Harry Oaks's face. There were indications that the bloodstains on the glass door and the screen door of Christie's bedroom may have come from his own hand after he had found Sir Harry. The prosecution did not center in on trying to link Harold Christie at all with the murder, but instead took his version at face value. One of the stranger tales that came out in the evidence, was that a Captain Seers, who was an assistant superintendent of police, claimed that on the night of the murder he had seen a station wagon with Christie sitting in the front seat and someone else driving. This had been contradicted by Christie, who claimed that he had never left the Oaks estate that evening. The strongest argument in the prosecution's case that was used to link the alleged murderer, Fred Marigny, to the murder of Harry Oaks was the fingerprint that Captain Barker claimed to have found in the bedroom.

In the 1940s it was a common practice to take fingerprints. The particular fingerprint in question, however, had not been photographed. Officer Barker claimed that it had not been possible to take a photograph since he had left his camera behind in Florida. Couldn't Barker have borrowed a camera from someone else? If Barker did need a camera from Florida why didn't he order one, so a photograph of the fingerprint could adequately have been shot? There were a great many questions on Barker's handling of the vital fingerprinting process that left the police's investigation open to challenge. The Captain claimed that he proceeded to take prints from the scene of the crime by lifting them onto scotch tape. Once he ran out of the tape he explained that he had lifted them on a patch of rubber which destroyed the original fingerprint. What was interesting was that after the fingerprints were taken it was Barker's claim that he had forgotten all about the one on the screen for ten days. It was only then after he had remembered about it that he examined and found that it was Marigny's print. Why would Barker forget about a fingerprint when he believed that such evidence would be vital in the proof of his case? Why did it take ten days for him to process the fingerprints at all?

Barker testified that the print came from a particular place on the screen. It turned out that the print did not come from the place that Barker indicated. His accuracy was certainly open to question since he also testified that certain lines drawn on the screen had not been made by him that on closer inspection turned out to be marked with his initials. The fingerprint itself seemingly was confusing in that a person could not clearly make out which way the finger was even pointing. What was even more questionable was the timing of the finding of the fingerprint. Supposedly, the Miami police claimed that the only access Marigny would have had to the screen was on the night of the murder. Evidence turned up, however, that Marigny had been taken upstairs at the Oaks home, known as Westborn, to be interviewed on the very day that Barker went through the fingerprinting process. Earlier in time, testimony had been given in a Magistrates court that Marigny had gone in after the fingerprinting processes had taken place. At the trial, other witnesses came forward with different testimony from the earlier hearing at the Magistrate court. It seems that Marigny had been taken upstairs between 11:00 A.M. and noon. This would have made it possible for Marigny to have been present at a time when the fingerprints could have been taken. Now, the police seemed to be backtracking by claiming that there may have been a mistake about the time. The defense made quite a bit about the convenience of the mistake. Marigny's defense counsel gave the indication that he had been taken upstairs for the express purpose of getting his fingerprint taken.

An interesting sidelight that came out in the case was the way the fingerprint actually looked. It seemed that the screen where the fingerprint was taken had a particular background. When the fingerprint was viewed the background from the screen did not show up. Arguably, the fingerprint should have the same background as the screen. Could the fingerprint instead have been taken off a glass of water, for example, that had been offered by the police to Fred Marigny? Did the police purposely take the fingerprint off of the glass and claim it had been taken off the screen in order to direct suspicion toward Marigny? The questions surrounding the taking of the fingerprint seriously undermined the prosecution's case.

Marigny, in testifying on his own behalf at trial, explained that the singed hairs on his beard and forearm had been caused when he lit a cigar over a candle. His testimony appeared credible and his demeanor was relaxed. The prosecution's case appeared weak when it went to the jury. It was probably not surprising that the jury's vote came to 9 - 3 for acquittal. The one thing they unanimously agreed on, however, is that there be a recommendation that Marigny be deported from the Bahamas. Fred Marigny won his case, but was forced out of paradise.

The Harry Oaks case remains unsolved, although there are possible solutions that have been proposed. Murders usually do not take place in a vacuum. The surrounding circumstances and timing may be good indicators of who would have motivation to commit a murder. Could a gambling group have felt it necessary to kill Sir Harry Oaks in order to remove their major obstacle?

It is possible that Harry Oaks may have been killed accidently and that his body had been burned in an attempt to cover up that evidence. A theory has developed that Harry Oaks attended a meeting earlier in the evening with a financial interest group who wanted to bring gambling to the Bahamas. Perhaps he was the unidentified individual allegedly seen traveling in a car with Christie near the time of the murder. In the midst of the business discussion, an altercation allegedly occurred and Harry was hit upon the head. The theory goes on to say that once Harry had incurred his head injuries he was brought back to his own home. The claim has been made that a vital witness disappeared who observed a boat being brought up to a dock at about the time that Harry's body would have been brought back to the estate. Once there, the bed was set on fire to cover up the unfortunate circumstances so that the evidence would not point to the people attending the meeting. The question arises where the flammable substance came from that set the fire. Why wasn't Harry's body more effectively set fire to and destroyed? On the night that Harry Oaks was killed could wind and possibly water from a tremendous storm have put out the fire in his room? The complex theory over a series of events starting with Harry Oaks being seriously hurt in an altercation and an attempted cover-up of his assault by a fire is based primarily upon speculation without sufficient evidence to support it.

Could a group of native Bahamians who felt that Harry Oaks was exerting too much power in the Bahamas have brought about his death? The use of fire and the fact that there were feathers in the bedroom may have tended to indicate a killer with a special way of committing the crime. Nevertheless, there is not strong evidence that a native independence movement in the Bahamas had sufficient bad feeling toward Harry Oaks to kill him. To the contrary, there were many people who admired the assistance that Harry Oaks had rendered to the Bahama Islands. He had been a leading contributor and did not have the kind of negative presence that would have led to a desire to kill him by a native Bahamian group.

Can Fred Marigny be totally excluded from possible suspects because he was acquitted? Even the jury was not unanimous in the acquittal. Could it be that Marigny did, in fact, bear malice towards his father-in-law and decided to end his life? Was it simply the botched job of the investigation that got Marigny off rather than the truth of his innocence? It has been argued that the evidence was so weak that there is not sufficient evidence to believe that Fred Marigny would have committed the crime. Isn't it possible that an outsider may have committed the act simply to rob Sir Harry? There has always been the lurking question of what wealth Harry Oaks may have kept in and about the estate.

There are many theories as to who actually killed Sir Harry Oaks. The one thing that is clear is that Nassau did end up becoming a leading resort area where gambling attracted many tourists yearly. Harry Oaks's paradise became a worldwide center where people enjoy, at least for a short time, the beautiful area that Sir Harry Oaks loved so much. Nassau also has the distinction of being the place where the great unsolved murder mystery of who killed Sir Harry Oaks began and has yet to end.

4

Was Napoleon Bonaparte Murdered?

Napoleon Bonaparte stirred controversy both in life and in death. In his life he managed to move through the ranks of the French Army from an ordinary soldier from Corsica to a general. If that was not enough, he later became Emperor of France. Certainly, these accomplishments would be more than enough for any normal person to aspire to achieve in a lifetime. Napoleon was not, however, a normal person. He would not have gotten to be emperor without incredible drive and vision. So wide was his appetite for power, that at one time he swallowed up most of Western Europe through political machinations and military victories on the battlefield. The story of how Napoleon accomplished these important acts is well documented in history. What is not so well known, is whether Napoleon Bonaparte died naturally or was murdered.

Napoleon's reign over much of Western Europe finally ended when he was defeated on the battlefield and forced out of power. As part of the settlement after Napoleon's defeat, he was exiled to live his life on the island of Elba. Arrangements were made to provide for a comfortable existence for Napoleon on the island.

Napoleon Bonaparte was not satisfied with just being in a comfortable environment. His spirit remained restless for the power to lead and conquer. He managed to escape and build another French army. Once again Napoleon terrorized the aristocracy of Europe by being in control of an army. They decided to end the threat once and for all by defeating his new army.

The battle of Waterloo ended Napoleon's new bid for power. He was sent again into exile. This time Napoleon was sent to the remote and often inhospitable island of St. Helena where he was sentenced to spend his remaining days. British authorities watched over Napoleon on St. Helena to make sure that he did not escape to build another French army that would threaten peace in Europe. Even in captivity Napoleon presented a danger. Although the British may have looked at Napoleon as a potential military threat, the French ruling class feared even more that he might escape and once more topple the aristocracy.

Napoleon understood the political realities of his situation. He feared that he might be assassinated while imprisoned on the island of St. Helena. If he was stabbed or shot, the murder would be a cause of political uproar among the French people. If he was obviously murdered, then the British would be considered prime suspects of

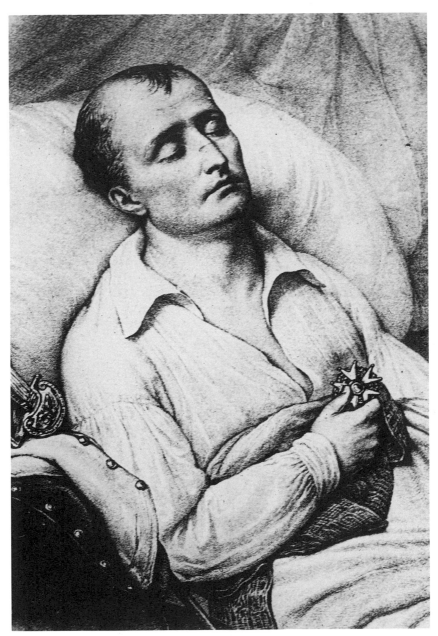

Napoleon Bonaparte on his death bed, 1821

political assassination. A French enemy would be very careful not to openly assassinate him since that would have a tendency to rally his former followers to again attack the ruling class of France. Poisoning Napoleon would be the simplest way to rid the world of him. Napoleon began to dwell on the possibility that he would be caught off guard and poisoned by one of his enemies.

In 1818, Napoleon exhibited symptoms of deep mental depression, sharp pains in the side of his body, and chronically cold feet. Although he complained about these problems, he did not get medical treatment that helped him. There began to be questions as to just what kind of care the British were providing to him. Unfortunately for Napoleon, he did not have the option to select, as he had earlier done as emperor, the type of medical aid that he wanted.

By the beginning of the year of 1821, Napoleon's illness became more severe. In talking with people, he gave the impression that he would not have long to live. His major concern was that he was being poisoned. At the same time, however, he maintained a nagging suspicion that he had cancer. Napoleon worried deeply that cancer might be hereditary, and that he would die of it as his father had at an early age. By 1821, Napoleon's sickness showed the additional symptoms of nausea, chills, a dry cough, and constant thirst. Possibly out of fear of poisoning or lack of faith in his doctors, he refused to take any medicines. Of course, it was possible that the medicines may have not have done him any good.

In the Will that Napoleon made out in the middle of April 1821, he stated that he wished that after his death an autopsy not be performed on his body. It seemed that he did not want any English physicians to become involved in reviewing his medical condition after death. Once again this may have indicated his belief that he was being politically assassinated by his former adversaries, the English. After undergoing a great deal of suffering the former Emperor of France passed away on May 5, 1821.

It was determined that Napoleon Bonaparte's autopsy would be performed by seven doctors. The Will that had been made was not strictly obeyed, as can be seen by the fact that six of the doctors were English. The doctors did not agree after exploration of Napoleon's body on what had caused his death. They found a growth in Napoleon's stomach that some doctors believed was cancerous. There were other physicians present, however, who questioned whether they had found cancer. There was the further question of whether the growth that was found inside Napoleon was the direct cause of the former Emperor of France's eventual death. Napoleon ended up in an inglorious and unmarked grave on St. Helena.

The political climate, however, began to shift in France in the years that passed after Napoleon's death. Nineteen years after his death, the sands of time had shifted the political alliances in such a way as to make Napoleon Bonaparte once more the hero of the French people. It was because of his renewed status as a hero that there was a determination that his body should be removed from St. Helena and reinterred in a massive burial monument in Paris.

When Napoleon's grave in St. Helena was opened the witnesses observed that his corpse was very well preserved. It seemed that he had not deteriorated substantially from how he had looked at death, while those that had stood by his grave nineteen years earlier had aged substantially in the years that had passed since then. How had Napoleon Bonaparte's corpse been able to stay in the remarkable state of condition when no special efforts had been made to preserve it before burial? If Napoleon Bonaparte's body had not been embalmed, why did he look so startlingly much like the day he had died? Some people argued that the four coffins his body was enclosed in was the key to the remarkable state of preservation. It was pointed out by doubters that if the coffins were not airtight they could not have allowed for the positive condition of Napoleon's body. Another explanation was that he had been poisoned with arsenic. Some people believe that although arsenic is a destructive poison, it could have acted as a preservative of Napoleon's tissue. Could Napoleon's body have acted as a positive witness that he was assassinated by arsenic poisoning? To this day, not everyone accepts the assertion that the state of Napoleon's bodily condition proves he was poisoned by arsenic. Some skeptics explain that even if the poison was present in his system, it may prove nothing more than Napoleon was an arsenic-eater. In the nineteenth century there were people who used arsenic as a form of drug. Over time they built up immunities so that they could handle larger quantities than the average person without death. If Napoleon was an arsenic-eater, then possibly the practice eventually caused his death.

Some people think Napoleon died from arsenic poisoning but do not accept that he was an arsenic-eater. They reason that he may have gotten poisoned by being exposed to materials around him that contained large doses of arsenic. For example, the wallpaper in his house may have contained arsenic. If Napoleon rubbed his fingers over the wallpaper and then touched his fingers to his tongue, it could cause arsenic poisoning. Could touching a substance with arsenic spread a sufficient dose of arsenic into the body to cause the severe symptoms that Napoleon exhibited?

When Napoleon died, rumors spread that he had been poisoned. There was not, however, sufficient evidence to back up this claim. Some people did not take the rumor of poisoning seriously since it was not uncommon to hear that a famous person died from poisoning. So often had this claim been made that many people discounted it in Napoleon's case and believed that he was just as vulnerable to death by natural causes as any other human being.

It wasn't until the 1950s that a Swedish dentist who was interested in Napoleon developed a firm theory that the former emperor's body exhibited definite indications of arsenic poisoning. It is difficult, however, to support the claim based upon the findings of the doctors at the autopsy. They published no proof that specific tests for arsenic were performed. There always is the possibility the English doctors performed the tests, but did not make the result public for fear of the consequences of the release of that information. In spite of the lack of information provided by the autopsy, the Swedish dentist pursued his theory. It was known in the 1950s that hair would retain arsenic. To determine the presence of arsenic, it was generally believed necessary to have a fairly substantial quantity of hair that could be tested. The dentist, however, was able to find someone at the University of Glasgow who had developed a test that could detect arsenic in a lone hair. A man in Paris was located who took an interest in the question presented on Napoleon's death and willingly turned over the hair necessary for testing.

After the test was performed, it was determined that Napoleon had been exposed to a large concentration of arsenic. The amount of arsenic detected was not necessarily enough to be fatal. It appeared as though the arsenic may have been administered over a fairly substantial amount of time. The data was also interpreted by some people as indicating that large doses had been administered at the times when Napoleon exhibited the worst outbreak of symptoms related to his illness. After the findings on the arsenic testing were published, a woman came forward with information on Napoleon's life on St. Helena. It appeared that the woman's ancestor had become a great friend of Napoleon's during his exile. From conversations that she had with him, her family strongly suspected that Napoleon had been poisoned. If Napoleon was poisoned, then who did it?

One way of finding the potential answer to the identity of the murderer was to find when Napoleon first exhibited the symptoms of his illness. If the timing of his symptoms could be connected with the introduction of a particular individual into his circle on St. Helena that might help single out the culprit. It seemed that a number of Napoleon's servants had loyally worked for him a long time. It would be unexpected for them to suddenly poison him. There was also no proof that any of his old servants harbored any resentment toward Napoleon.

When reviewing Napoleon's immediate household one suspect seemed to stand out above the others, a Count Charles Tristan De'Montholon. It seemed that he had been a born aristocrat, but had gone to St. Helena with Napoleon to act as his servant. The idea of an aristocrat giving up life in France in order to act as a servant to Napoleon seemed questionable. A review of Montholon's history showed that after Napoleon's defeat he had initially gone back to showing an allegiance to the Bourbons, who were the ruling family of France. He later chose to give up life in France and again rejoin Bonaparte in his exile on St. Helena. Certainly, Montholon's motivation seems cloudy and suspicious. There is no proof that he had ever been a tremendous supporter of Napoleon, so why after the emperor was defeated would an aristocrat give up a life in France to take on the job as a servant?

Montholon had the job of being in charge of Napoleon's house, which included regulating the food supply of the former emperor. This would give him access to providing and introducing a poison into the emperor's meals. Was Montholon specifically sent to St. Helena to assassinate Napoleon by the ruling class in France?

It seems that there was more than one part of the royal family that would have a motive for seeing to it that Napoleon's life was ended. Could the Count d'Artois, who was the brother of the deposed Louis XVI, have been behind the plot? After his brother, King Louis XVI was beheaded during the French Revolution, he harbored a great hatred for the commoners who took over control of what he believed to be his family's country. He especially developed an intense hatred of the person who usurped the throne, Napoleon Bonaparte. It was believed that while Napoleon was in exile the Count d'Artois, as brother of the former King Louis XVI, made a number of earlier plans to kill Napoleon that were unsuccessful. Could the Count d'Artois have finally pulled off a successful plan to polish off his arch enemy, Napoleon Bonaparte? Did he perform the active assassination through a hired aristocrat, Montholon? It seems that Montholon showed no apparent wealth and certainly may have been a candidate that was open to financial reward in exchange for getting rid of Napoleon Bonaparte through poisoning.

The Count d'Artois was to have his opportunity to rule France as King Charles X. Unlike Napoleon Bonaparte, he was not to win the people's favor. His reign over France was brief. He was driven out of power and forced into exile. The theory that Napoleon Bonaparte was poisoned by Montholon is interesting, but lacks documentation. A review of the documents of the former ruler of France, King Charles X, who might have been the instigator of the plot, does not show evidence that a plot had been hatched by him to use Montholon to poison Napoleon.

Could Napoleon have died from a tumor that was cancerous? It seems that Napoleon Bonaparte had experienced physical ailments before the alleged poisoning began. If Napoleon Bonaparte was poisoned by arsenic in the wall paper, then why weren't others in his household similarly affected? If the former emperor leaned against the wall and traced designs with his fingers and then placed them in his mouth, would he have received a sufficient dose of arsenic to cause his death? What proof do we have that Napoleon Bonaparte ever made contact with wallpaper that had arsenic in it?

It seems difficult to accept that charismatic leaders die like ordinary people. Is the theory of Napoleon Bonaparte's poisoning a product of the fact that a segment of the public wants to believe he would not have died of an ordinary kind of illness? The controversy surrounding Napoleon's death might be resolved if modern doctors could thoroughly investigate his remains. It seems unlikely that any such testing will ever take place, since the body of the Emperor Napoleon lays entombed in a solid structure that would not allow for his easy removal. Since Napoleon's body will probably never be taken out of its tomb, the question of his death will probably remain one more controversy about the great leader that will go on in succeeding generations.

5

Dr. Sam Sheppard

The sleepy town of Bay Village, Ohio, became the focus of nationwide attention after Marilyn Sheppard was found murdered there on July 4, 1954. She was the wife of Dr. Sam Sheppard who was a successful osteopath. At the time of Marilyn's death she was pregnant. The Sheppards had one son, Chip, who was seven years old. The evening before the murder, the Sheppards had another couple, who were friends, at their home. When the visitors left the Sheppard home, they observed Marilyn lock the front door leading to the lake. They did not, however, see if she locked the door that led to the road. What followed after the Sheppards' friends left their home has been the center of speculation since the brutalized body of Marilyn was found.

Dr. Sheppard's story was that he fell asleep on the

couch in the living room. He awakened in the early hours of the morning to hear his wife's screams. His response was to run quickly upstairs to render assistance.

Under the dim light, he saw the figure of a man dressed in white standing over his wife's bed. Sam was then knocked out. After reviving, he heard noises in his house and saw a figure dressed in white running down the lawn towards a beach house. He quickly pursued the mysterious person in white, who turned out to be a large man with bushy hair. After catching up with the figure a scuffle ensued and Sam Sheppard was again knocked out. Upon coming to consciousness, he found himself lying partly in water. In a confused state, he staggered back to his home to check on his wife. He knelt on the bed and checked Marilyn's condition by feeling her pulse. Sheppard then called a friend who was also the mayor of Bay Village. He explained that, "They've killed Marilyn," and urged his friend to quickly come over to his house.

When the mayor and his wife arrived a short time after receiving the call from Sam, the door facing the road was unlocked. Dr. Sheppard's medical bag was laying in the hallway, while he sat on a chair in the den. His face was swollen and he appeared ill. Sam had no shirt on and his pants appeared to be wet. He related the events of the early morning hours in his house. The mayor's wife ran upstairs and then hurriedly returned. She stressed the need to call the police and an ambulance.

Dr. Richard Sheppard, who was Sam's brother, was one of the early arrivals to the scene. After examining Marilyn he estimated that her death took place two hours previous to that time. She had apparently been severely beaten until she died. Her top garment was raised up

Dr. Sam Sheppard

which indicated that the killer either attempted rape or had a desire to terminate her pregnancy. When Richard went to wash his hands he noticed a regular cigarette butt floating in the toilet. Neither his brother nor his deceased sister-in-law allegedly smoked regular cigarettes of that brand. This was the first of many clues that were to be found at the scene of the crime.

Dr. Richard Sheppard found his brother was in great physical discomfort. In spite of that fact, Richard asked Sam, if he had anything to do with his wife's murder. Sam shot back an unhesitant, "No," to the question. When the Police Chief arrived, Sam repeated his story about being hit in the bedroom and later struggling outside his house with the bushy-haired man. Dr. Steven Sheppard, another brother of Sam's who had recently arrived, concluded after examination that his brother may have incurred an injury to his spinal cord. He arranged to have Sam taken to a hospital that was owned and operated by the Sheppard family. Once there it was observed that Sam's skin looked as though he had been submerged in water for some time. It appeared to some observers as though he was in a state of shock. His lips were cut and his upper right teeth were loose.

After arriving at the hospital, he was interrogated at about 9:00 A.M. by the Cuyahoga County Corner, Dr. Sam Gerber. Then again at 11:00 A.M. he was questioned by two Cleveland detectives. By this time it was clear from the detectives' questioning that they had centered their suspicion on Dr. Sam Sheppard as the killer. The law enforcement officers in charge of the investigation, believed that Sam's version of what had happened in the early morning hours of the murder was ridiculous. They were not shy in presenting their theory of the events surrounding the murder. According to them, Dr. Sheppard allegedly quarreled with his wife and murdered her in a rage. He washed his wife's blood off of himself in the lake and faked a burglary in his home to give credence to the idea that an outsider had committed the murder. Sam allegedly wiped off fingerprints and blood left by him at the scene of the crime. He also hid incriminating evidence. Dr. Sheppard supposedly injured himself purposely by falling down the stairs to the beach.

Sam Sheppard's story was not accepted by the Cleveland, Ohio newspapers. They continually hammered home to the public the need for strong action against the murderer. The newspapers acted as investigators, prosecutors, judge, and jury of Sam Sheppard's guilt. The effect of the repeated publicity was to give the impression that Sam Sheppard was clearly the murderer and that the only thing that kept him from being arrested was his social prominence and wealth. Dr. Sam Sheppard was tried and found guilty in the newspapers.

Sam was arrested for murder and his trial started on October 18, 1954. Sheppard's trial proved to be more of a circus than a legal proceeding in search of truth. The judge in the case appeared to take a tremendous amount of interest in catering to the needs of the press. He expressed to a reporter of national prominence by the name of Dorothy Killgallen, that he was surprised that she was sent all the way to Cleveland when it appeared to be an open and shut case since Sam Sheppard was guilty.

It was evident that both the Cleveland law enforcement authorities and local press had a prejudice toward the defendant. In spite of requests by the defense, Sam Sheppard's attorney had not even had an opportunity to go through the Sheppard home to inspect evidence at the actual crime scene. This proved to be a real disadvantage during the trial. The case against the defendant was based largely upon evidence that the prosecution had taken out of the Sheppard home. Without access to the home, counsel for the defense could not fully introduce expert testimony to refute the prosecution's version of what the Sheppard home showed about the events surrounding Marilyn's murder.

The prosecution argued that the reason why no shirt was found on Sam Sheppard after the murder was that he had gotten blood on it. He discarded the shirt because it was incriminating evidence against him. Coroner Gerber claimed that the bloodstain found on the knee of Dr. Sheppard's wet pants proved he had murdered his wife. The defense's explanation was that Sam did not know what happened with his tee shirt, but that the stain on the knee of his pants probably was caused when he knelt down to check his wife's pulse. Investigators of the murder had found on the Sheppard property a bag with a bloodstained wristwatch which was stopped shortly after 4:00 A.M., Dr. Sheppard's fraternity ring, and a key ring. The police believed that the bag was planted in a clumsy attempt by Dr. Sheppard to try and indicate that a burglary had taken place in his home. Nevertheless, they did not show that adequate attempts had been made by them to fingerprint the objects that had been found at the crime scene. The prosecution seemed to justify their inattention to detail by claiming that Sam had wiped everything in the house clean in order to destroy fingerprint evidence and cleaned up the traces of blood that would have indicated his guilt.

One of the major points that the prosecution made was that they had found a large bloodstain on Marilyn's pillow. Dr. Gerber believed that the stain showed the imprint of a double-pronged surgical instrument. He did not, however, explain what exact instrument would leave such an imprint. The blood splatters on the wall of the death room were seemingly ignored by the prosecution. Instead the alleged blood trail on the stairs was emphasized. The prosecution seemed to reason that Dr. Sheppard had murdered his wife and then left bloodstains as he traveled down the stairs. They ignored the possibility that the bloodstains may not have been made by Sam and that an intruder could have just as easily left the stains. Much was seemingly made out of the prosecution's claim that Dr. Sheppard had trivial injuries that could have been caused by himself. They argued that Sheppard, as a part of his cover-up, damaged himself slightly in order to give support to his claim that he had been hurt by an outside intruder.

The prosecution's presentation cleverly painted a picture of Sam Sheppard as a Dr. Jekyll and Mr. Hyde type of person. On the surface he seemed to be a caring doctor, but down deep was deceitful and brutal. The prosecution gave the impression that, while in a terrible rage, Sam beat his wife to death and then covered it up. The most damaging evidence that was introduced by the prosecution, however, was the introduction of a woman witness who claimed to have had an affair with Dr. Sheppard during his marriage to the victim. The effect of this revelation on the spectators in the courtroom was tremendous.

The focus of the attention shifted from the evidence that was found at the scene of the crime to Dr. Sheppard's morality. The introduction of evidence of Sam's love affair with another woman during the marriage gave the impression that Sam Sheppard was not an honest person and that he may have been motivated to kill his wife, in order to be able to live with another woman.

Sam's defense stressed that the case against him was based on ambiguous evidence that did not prove he was the killer. Emphasis was put on the Sam's injuries, to show he was a victim rather than the murderer. A doctor testified that Sam had received spinal damage and a dentist testified he had received damage to his teeth. Both doctors seemed to believe that the type of injuries that Sheppard incurred were not consistent with being self-inflicted. When it became obvious, however, that Sam could not defend against the testimony that he had been adulterous it seemed that his credibility was lost. Would the jury's deliberation be influenced more by the testimony that Sam had committed adultery than the actual evidence found at the scene of the crime?

After five days of deliberation, the jury returned its verdict, that Sam Sheppard was guilty of second degree murder. This meant that they accepted that Sam had intentionally killed his wife, but had not found sufficient proof that he had planned the crime before doing it to warrant a verdict of first degree murder.

The Cleveland press was elated with the news of Sam Sheppard's conviction. In an attempt to prepare for an appeal of the decision, Sam's lawyer again asked the judge for a chance to get into the Sheppard home. Finally, he was given the keys to the Sheppard home, so that he would have the opportunity to carefully review the scene of the crime. A famous criminologist from California, Dr. Paul Kirk, was retained to inspect the home and review the evidence for the defense. He meticulously went through the crime scene. He took photographs, measurements, and even reconstructed a small scale model of the Sheppards' bedroom. After exhaustive testing of the evidence, his conclusions indicated great weaknesses in the technical evidence that had earlier been presented by the prosecution at trial.

Dr. Kirk believed that, if the initial blow that struck against Marilyn had been vertical, as indicated by the prosecution, then the ceiling should have shown bloodstains. Since there were no such stains on the ceiling, the logical conclusion was that Marilyn had been hit by horizontal swings, which had caused the blood marks on the walls of the bedroom. The pattern of the bloodstains on the wall and Marilyn's body position tended to show that the person who delivered the murderous blows was left handed. Dr. Sam Sheppard, however, was a right handed person, which again showed a significant weakness in the prosecution's position.

Dr. Gerber testified that he believed the murder weapon was a surgical double-pronged instrument, but Dr. Kirk did not find evidence to support the coroner's theory. The defense expert reasoned that the injuries were not likely to have been caused by a medical instrument, but rather from an object that was not more than one foot long that had a flared front edge, such as would be expected on a heavy flashlight. A red spot of lacquer that was found at the scene that some people thought was nail polish was reviewed by Dr. Kirk. He found that it could have been a piece of red lacquer such as was used to coat smaller objects such as a flashlight. The red chip may have come off after contact between a flashlight and Marilyn's body. Possibly, the portable light had been brought into the bedroom to illuminate it, but later was used as the murder weapon. It even may have been used to knock out Sam Sheppard.

Chemical analysis of the scene showed that there was a spot of human blood near a closet of the murder room that did not match the blood type of either Dr. Sheppard or his deceased wife. To Dr. Kirk, this indicated that the blood may have been from an intruder. Marilyn's teeth may have been broken by the unknown person who left the bloodstain. The prosecution gave the impression that the teeth had been broken by a blow delivered to Mrs. Sheppard's mouth. This was not consistent with the evidence. If the blow was delivered from the outside then Marilyn Sheppard's teeth should have been knocked inward. In this case, the teeth were found outside the body which was consistent with the theory that they had been pulled forcefully outward, possibly when the unknown intruder pulled his or her hand out of the area of Marilyn's mouth. The murderer could have covered up Marilyn's mouth and have been bit by her in the process of trying to break free. As the intruder pulled his or her hand outward, it broke Mrs. Sheppard's teeth. The bloodstains in the area of the closet could have been from the killer's injured hand. If Sam Sheppard had been the murderer then there should have been evidence that his hand had been bitten. On July 4, 1954, no bite mark was observed on Sam Sheppard's hands.

Dr. Kirk believed the four-inch rip on Sam's pants was

consistent with the idea that someone other than he created it. He found that it would have been physically impossible for Sam to have torn his own trouser pocket downward to remove the key chain because of the extreme movement that it would have taken to move upward and outward.

The leather products worn by Sam Sheppard, such as his belt, showed no bloodstains under the study of a microscope. If Sam had committed the murder, then the blood splatter would have gone into the leather, which could not have been cleaned thoroughly enough to remove all remnants of the blood.

Consistent with Sam's story about being knocked out after a struggle by the lake was the fact that his pants pockets contained approximately two tablespoons of sand. The contents of Sam's pockets supported the idea that he was lying in the water for at least an hour.

Given Dr. Kirk's evidentiary findings and reconstruction of the crime, he was able to make conclusions as to what happened on the terrible night of the murder. He reasoned that if Dr. Sheppard had removed a bloody tee shirt himself then he would have certainly put another one on. It did not make sense that Sam would have made such a clumsy attempt at faking a burglary attempt to cover up a murder. If he was to do that then why make his story so vague and open to question. The clumsy ripping action of the pants in order to get access to the key chain was not consistent with a well thought out plan by Sheppard. The athletic trophies of Sam and his wife had been intentionally broken. If Sam Sheppard was trying to fake the crime scene, it would not be necessary for him to do such damage. The fact that the trophies were broken was more likely to have been caused by a jealous intruder. Why would Sam Sheppard destroy his own athletic trophies?

The injuries that Sam Sheppard incurred seemed inconsistent with the idea that they were self-inflicted. Certainly, a doctor realizing the danger of an injury to the neck would never purposely risk a blow to it. Sam's injuries did not appear to be the type that would have been caused by purposely falling from a platform. Had he fallen in such a manner, then there certainly would have been bruises and abrasions on his body.

The evidence and related conclusions from Dr. Kirk were presented to the trial Judge Bylthin. The judge decided that the evidence presented was not compelling enough to order a new trial. Sam's attorney appealed the judge's decision all the way through the Ohio court system, but was unsuccessful in getting an order for a new trial. The defense was not, however, easily dissuaded in following its goal, and took a petition all the way up to the United States Supreme Court asking that the conviction be reversed. The defense's petition contained examples of the prejudice that was shown to Sam's case by the sensationalist newspaper publicity that was adverse to him. It was the contention of the defense that Sam Sheppard had been denied due process of law as set forth by the 14th Amendment to the United States Constitution. The United States Supreme Court, however, did not accept the controversial Sheppard case for review at that time.

A non-profit organization that went by the name of Court of Last Resort, was founded in the late 1940s by Earl Stanley Gardner, who was the creator of Perry Mason.

The refusal of the United States Supreme Court to review the Sheppard case prompted a relative of Sam Sheppard's to write the Court of Last Resort to see if they would investigate the Sheppard murder case. After going through their own independent investigation, the experts who were called in by the Court of Last Resort believed that there was potentially a definite weakness in the case against Sam Sheppard. In his writings, Gardner made magazine readers aware of the situation and that they could write the state of Ohio in order to see to it that Sam Sheppard was allowed to take a lie detector test. Ohio officials lashed out against Earl Stanley Gardner and the Court of Last Resort. They claimed that the informal body was wrongfully interfering with the case after the courts in Ohio and the United States Supreme Court had already passed on the subject. In response, the Court of Last Resort withdrew from actively pursuing a further course of investigation on the case.

After the defense attorney who had handled the original jury trial died in 1961, a new attorney entered the scene to assist Sam Sheppard. He used a different approach to handling Sam's case. A habeas corpus petition was filed on April 11, 1963, in the United States District Court for the Southern District of Ohio. It set forth that Sam Sheppard's fundamental constitutional rights had been denied him in the way the judge, prosecution, and even the press handled themselves during the trial. Sam's new lawyer cited a number of errors by the court. Special emphasis was put on the charge that Sam Sheppard had been denied a fair trial by the extraordinarily adverse publicity by the press. A federal court ruled that Sam Sheppard's constitutional rights had been violated and that he should be released upon the posting of a bond. In essence, the federal court judge ruled that Sam Sheppard was denied a fair trial as required by the due process clause of the 14th Amendment. It did not mean that the judge was deciding that Sam Sheppard was innocent or guilty, but rather that he had not received a fair trial as set forth in the United States Constitution. The prosecution appealed the case to the Federal Court of Appeals. That court overruled Judge Wyman, the lower court federal judge, and ordered that Sam Sheppard return to the penitentiary. This time, however, the United States Supreme Court determined that they would review the case. In its landmark decision, the Supreme Court ruled that Sam Sheppard had received an unfair trial in 1954. They did not decide that Sam Sheppard was either guilty or innocent, but rather that the atmosphere and pressure by the press deprived Sheppard of a fair trial. It seems that the court also recognized that the trial judge had not ensured that Sam's case was treated fairly and impartially. No doubt what the trial judge told Dorothy Killgallen at the time of the trial about Sam Sheppard's guilt was a significant indicator of the lack of impartiality by the Court.

Further, the fact that media representatives were allowed to have their own table inside the court showed the interest and prejudicial advantage that was given to the press at trial. By having the press take such a prominent role they, in effect, could greatly impact and affect the witnesses, law enforcement, and even the prosecution's performance during presentation of the case. The Supreme Court opinion did not attempt to harm the power of the press, but simply to balance the system so that the Court protected the constitutional rights of an accused person who was charged with a crime and proceeding through trial. As a result of the denial of a fair trial, the Supreme Court decided that Sam Sheppard was to be allowed a new trial.

In the fall of 1966, Sam Sheppard started his new trial. This time, however, it was not to be a field day for the press, but a straight-forward examination of the facts. The prosecution did not have the advantage of having exclusive control of evidence from the crime scene. Dr. Gerber, the coroner, who had been so effective at the first trial in pointing a finger at Dr. Sheppard came across very poorly under the scathing attack of defense counsel. Although he had claimed that the bloodstained pillow showed that the victim had been murdered with a medical weapon, he could not pinpoint just what surgical instrument supposedly delivered the fatal blows. The comments that were made by the coroner before the first trial showed that he was prejudiced against the Sheppard family.

Through further cross-examination of a prosecution witness the defense was able to get out the fact that it appeared that the weapon that delivered the fatal blows was swung in a left handed arc. This showed another weakness in the prosecution's case, since Sam Sheppard was right-handed.

Probably the more significant points put forward by the defense were delivered by Dr. Paul Kirk, who came to testify as to his findings. This time he was allowed to explain the conclusions that he had made way back in the middle 1950s in making his post-trial affidavit. The defendant Sam Sheppard did not testify at the second trial, which may have strengthened his position. When the case went to the jury, the prosecution had only a thin set of accusations that had been greatly weakened by the cross-examination of the defense counsel and the evidence presented through its expert witness, Dr. Kirk. The second jury returned with a verdict of not guilty.

The Sheppard case stands as a milestone in the annals of justice. It established the importance of balancing the right of freedom of the press with the rights of an accused. The decision did not, however, win Sam Sheppard freedom from the suspicions and accusations of his peers. Sam tried to go back to being a doctor, but could not maintain a successful medical practice. He ended up working as a professional wrestler. When Sam passed away in 1970, some people still questioned whether or not he was guilty of murdering his wife Marilyn.

6

The Mysterious Death of William Taylor

On the morning of February 1, 1922, movie studio executives in Los Angeles, California, viewed a handsome, middle-aged man lying with his back to the floor and his arms neatly placed at his sides. The facial features of that person showed the restful expression of sleep. His clothes were neatly arranged to fit the picture of what would be expected of a suave, sophisticated man's wardrobe. Near one of the legs of his body was a turned-over chair. The setting was not one of make believe created for the silver screen, but rather the real locale where the dead body of the famous motion picture director, William Desmond Taylor, was found. Although the scene was not for a movie, it had all of the artistic creativity that would be expected of the finest theatrical mind.

Taylor's dead body had been found earlier that morning by his valet, Henry Peavey. Following the discovery of the body, the distraught valet had run out of the home screaming that his employer was dead. Upon hearing the news, neighbors made calls to people who had connections with the dead man. Within a short time the Taylor home was bustling with visitors.

Executives from the movie studio where Taylor worked went through the house searching for evidence that might cast a negative light upon their business. The heads of the studio were very concerned with the possibility that adverse publicity might hurt their business if anything was found in the Taylor home that made one of their directors or actors look as though they were not wholesome.

The famous movie star, Mable Normand, was also at the dead director's home that morning searching for love letters that she had sent him. One of the more unusual visitors, was a doctor who was found nearby. He came into the home and after a brief inspection announced that Taylor had died from natural causes. It was only later when a coroner arrived at the scene and turned over the body that the real cause of death became known. He observed that there was a bloodstain on the carpet. Under Taylor's left arm was a bullet hole. There was another wound in his back. It appeared that William Taylor had been shot with a single .38 caliber bullet, which had passed through his heart and exited through his back.

Why didn't the earlier doctor find the clear indications that Taylor had been shot? Could the mysterious doctor

William Taylor, 1922

have purposely tried to keep out the truth of how the director died? This was not the only thing that was confusing about the scene of Taylor's death. In many cases there is a lack of evidence, but the Taylor home may have had too many clues. When Taylor's servant Henry Peavey found the director's body early that morning it started one of the more bizarre and complex murder investigations in history.

After the police started their investigations they were still able to find indications of relationships that Taylor had with women who were publicly known to movie-goers, despite the fact that movie people had earlier had a chance to try and sanitize the Taylor home. Among the famous director's belongings were found letters from the comedian and actress, Mary Miles Minter. In the toe of one of Taylor's boots was hidden the love letter of another star, Mable Normand. Investigators even found women's clothing in a locked compartment within a locked chest.

It seemed that what was found at the director's house supported the reputation Taylor had earned of being a playboy. Why hadn't the movie people found the revealing personal items when they were cleaning up the murder scene? Could it be that what was found was not necessarily there before the murder? Could the evidence of Taylor's many love affairs have been props left by the movie people? Evidence could have been planted to distract investigators from looking at the proper suspect.

The wounds on Taylor's body presented another perplexing problem. It seemed that the bullet holes in the body did not line up with his jacket. This gave rise to a question of just what had happened in the moments that preceded his death. The theory was that William Taylor had his arms raised at the time he was shot, which would have brought his jacket higher when the bullet penetrated the body. When his arms were later lowered to a position next to his body the holes in the clothing would not match up with the bodily wounds. Since William Taylor's body was placed so neatly on the ground with the arms to the side, it would imply that the killer or someone else afterwards purposely arranged the body in the way that it was found. Another theory was that William Taylor had been seated at his desk when the killer approached him. As the director was leaning forward to write, with his left arm extended to hold the paper, he was shot. Did the killer wait for Taylor to sign something before executing him?

The police gathered through their initial investigation that William Taylor had met with his friend Mable Normand the night of his murder. When Ms. Normand first arrived she heard him arguing with someone over the telephone and the conversation ended abruptly. She stayed for a short while with Taylor and then left. The police found inside the director's home nearly one thousand dollars in cash. Taylor even had seventy-eight dollars in his pocket. A number of cigarette butts were found outside the back door. Observers in the neighborhood claimed to have seen someone leave the Taylor home in the evening hours after Mable Normand's departure. It seemed a key witness recalled that the person leaving the director's house appeared to be a man wearing a cap and a long coat, that walked like a woman.

The police looked into William Desmond Taylor's past in order to try to find a suspect who would have been motivated to commit the murder. They found evidence that the director's personality was far more exciting and complex than would be even expected from a character depicted in a movie. It seems that William Desmond Taylor was an alias for William Cunningham Deane Tanner, who was born in County Cork, Ireland, in 1877. His family was wealthy and had a tradition of service in the military. After attending school as a young person William Tanner became rebellious and joined a theater company. He left the conservative lifestyle of his ancestors to become an actor. Later his restless spirit caused him to travel to the United States where he pursued a number of different occupations. In New York City he operated, along with his brother, a very prestigious and successful antique business. He was married to an attractive actress from a well-to-do background.

For an unexplained reason, Taylor left his flourishing business, wife, and only child to continue his travels in October of 1908. It seems that William Tanner, alias Taylor, followed an odyssey of adventure for the next five years throughout the United States and Canada. During this time he worked for a while in hotel management and as a prospector. He ended up working in Hollywood as an actor before World War I. He later left the movie capital to serve as a Captain in the Canadian Army during World War I. During his time in the military Taylor allegedly got another soldier in a great deal of trouble by reporting him for dishonesty. The soldier swore that he would someday get even with Taylor.

After the war, he returned to Hollywood to start a career as a film director. At this time he had a valet by the name of Edward Sands, who was later to become a leading suspect in the murder. It seems that in 1921 while Taylor was out of town, his valet took advantage of the situation by forging checks in Taylor's name, using his credit without permission, and stealing his property. When Taylor learned of the valet's dishonesty their relationship ended with Sands being fired. Could Taylor's former valet have murdered him because of a grudge? The police were later to search for the elusive Sands in an attempt to question him to see if he had any role in bringing about the death of his former employer. California authorities, however, were not successful in finding enough information to determine what, if any, role Sands had in the murder.

After World War I, Taylor had been joined in California by his brother, Dennis, who played a limited role in the burgeoning Hollywood movie community. Dennis had also left his wife and children in New York. Did he leave the antique business because he had a wanderlust or was he forced to do so because he no longer had his brother's expertise to keep the business going? After the Taylor murder there was some speculation that Dennis may have been the same person as the valet. The allegation that Dennis Tanner played the role of Sands the valet has never been substantiated.

As a director, William Taylor came into contact with some of the leading women stars in Hollywood. In the course of his direction, he had an opportunity to meet Mary Pickford, Mary Miles Minter, and Mable Normand. It was the latter two stars, however, who developed personal relationships with the director. Mable Normand even visited with the famous director at his home on the night of the murder, February 1, 1922. She left the Taylor

89

home at about 7:45 P.M. There were allegations that the female star had a drug habit and that Taylor had acted as her protector. The story had circulated around Hollywood that he had warned off drug pushers who had been supplying his friend's habit. Evidence found at the scene of the murder gave proof to the idea that Mable Normand probably had a love interest in Taylor. There was speculation that Mable Normand was jealous over Taylor's attention to his other girlfriend Mary Miles Minter.

William Taylor may also have aggravated Mable Normand because he presented a danger to her career by interfering with her secret drug use. She may have feared that the public would learn of his effort to keep drug pushers away from her. If her drug habit became public knowledge, then her career would be destroyed. It had been said that Taylor had even gone so far as to pay a visit to a prosecuting attorney's office to reveal information.

Could acute anxiety caused by Taylor's relationships with other women and paranoia about public exposure of her drug habit have motivated Mable Normand, when she was under the influence of drugs, to commit Taylor's murder? Although Mable Normand's participation in the director's murder was never substantiated by the evidence, the public made its own decision when the papers connected her with Taylor. Afterwards, movie-goers stayed away from her movies. She eventually was washed up as an actress in the movies.

The other major film star who, after the murder, was connected with William Taylor by the press also experienced a decline in her career. There was speculation that the blond hair allegedly found on Taylor's clothing was from Mary Miles Minter. After the 1922 murder her name was linked with the Taylor murder whenever there was mention of suspects.

Mary Miles Minter was not the only person in her family who had contact with the famous director. Her mother, Charlotte Shelby, had dealings with William Taylor, while helping with her daughter's career. She exerted strict control over Mary's daily life, in order to keep her daughter's image as a young wholesome actress. The types of parts that Mary Miles Minter starred in called for her to appear to be a fresh young girl. Shelby feared that her daughter's career would be destroyed if Mary was linked with a well-known playboy. Since she was so dependent financially upon a share of her daughter's earnings, she resented any love relationship between her offspring and William Taylor.

There has been speculation that Charlotte Shelby was also jealous over Taylor's attention to her daughter. One theory that connects the two women to the murder is that on the night of the murder it became apparent to Charlotte Shelby that her daughter might be getting out of her tight control and possibly establishing an open love relationship with Taylor. Out of fear of loss of control over her daughter, Charlotte Shelby went to the director's home to confront him. That evening Mable Normand was visiting with Taylor, while his other love interest, Mary Miles Minter, was upstairs in the home waiting for him to conclude his discussions with Normand. The theory is that Charlotte Shelby waited outside the back door of the Taylor home while he talked to Mable Normand. She did not know that her daughter was already inside the home. Could the cigarette butts found outside the back door have been left by Charlotte Shelby?

It is believed that she was smoking outside to kill time until she could privately confront the man who challenged the authority she held over her daughter. Once Mable Normand left, Shelby entered the home and shot the director with a .38 caliber gun. Mary Miles Minter may have been a witness to the event and contributed to arranging his body in a neat manner. Could Charlotte Shelby have been the person who was observed leaving the home? Shelby could have disguised herself as a man by wearing a large coat and pulling a cap down to cover her face. What she either forgot about or could not fully disguise was her feminine walk.

What about the alleged claims that both a man and a woman were observed leaving the scene of the murder? Could Charlotte Shelby have appeared to be a male figure with the big coat, and Mary Miles Minter a female? Shelby supposedly successfully avoided prosecution by payoffs in key places. Although the theory presents an interesting approach to tying together loose ends in the case, it is not strong enough to prove beyond a reasonable doubt that Charlotte Shelby murdered William Taylor.

There are other explanations for what happened on the night of the murder. William Taylor supposedly had a number of love relationships. After Mable Normand left his home, a jealous lover may have killed him. The killer could also have been a man with a grudge. Couldn't the Canadian soldier, who resented the problems Taylor had caused him, have committed the murder? Even Taylor's former valet Sands could have been the killer. Couldn't

Taylor's brother Dennis have been motivated to kill him out of resentment over his earlier abandonment of the antique business in New York and jealousy of his later success in Hollywood as a director?

Even if Mable Normand was not directly responsible for the murder, there is always a question about the drug pushers who were confronted by Taylor. Could a drug dealer have killed Taylor to keep him quiet? Is it hard to accept that a drug dealer might want to eliminate a person who would interfere with his sales to the increasingly wealthy movie set?

Blackmail maybe a possible explanation for the eventual demise of William Desmond Taylor. The famous director supposedly maintained strong feelings against blackmail. Could it be that Taylor did not have the wanderlust that has been credited to him, but was forced to flee at times because of blackmail? When Mable Normand got to his home he apparently was on the telephone arguing with someone. Could it be that a blackmailer was on the other end of the telephone? After Taylor's murder it turned out that he had been reviewing his financial situation before he was shot. A day earlier he had withdrawn $2,500 from the bank, but redeposited it the day of his murder. Could Taylor have first withdrawn the money in order to make a payoff and then changed his mind and redeposited it because he was finally going to take a stand against the blackmailer? Was Taylor murdered by a blackmailer who no longer found a willing victim?

The many possible twists and turns in the Taylor case make for a fascinating mystery, with clues that may never allow for an absolute solution to who committed the murder. No Hollywood film ever had more interesting characters, a better plot and more tantalizing clues. In the best tradition of Hollywood, Taylor left a story that not only captures people's interest, but keeps them coming back to review the story. It is too bad that William Taylor had to be an actual victim to create one of the great mystery stories of all time.

7

The Black
Dahlia

On January 15, 1947, the mutilated body of a young woman was found in an open area in Los Angeles on South Norton Avenue near 39th Street. The police later found that the woman was known as the Black Dahlia. Although her murder has not been solved, it is said that over 500 people have admitted to having been the culprit. The murder case has taken on legendary status and become something of a cult mystery. Why has the Black Dahlia murder mystery generated enduring public interest? Possibly, it may have something to do with the background of the woman who bore the unusual title of the Black Dahlia.

In the process of investigating the murder the police found that the Black Dahlia's real name was Elizabeth Short. Her beginnings were less than glamorous. She had been born in Medford, Massachusetts, and ran away from home at the age of seventeen to avoid what she believed to have been a dull life. Elizabeth was one of the glamour seekers who was attracted to the Hollywood of the mid-twentieth century. These young people, much as the modern-day runaways, felt the magnetic pull of movieland. Elizabeth, otherwise known as Beth, dreamt of someday becoming a star. When she first arrived in California in 1943, she felt the lure of Hollywood, but found that breaking into the movies was not an easy thing to do. There were hundreds of other young women just like her with talent. She would have to compete against them in order to even have an opportunity for a small part.

To provide for her financial needs, she took a job at an air force base north of Los Angeles working in a PX. Although she had proved quite popular with the men at the base, her wanderlust sent her off to Santa Barbara where she ended up getting arrested for drinking under age. It was here that the police took mugshots and fingerprints which later were used for the purposes of identification. After her bad experiences in California, she returned to Boston, Massachusetts, where she tried a more traditional lifestyle. Once again she became dissatisfied with the mundane job of working in a restaurant and ended up heading for the warm and glamorous climate of Miami, Florida. Even the beautiful weather in Florida was not enough to keep Elizabeth Short in one place. After stays in various places, she ended up following a route across the country that eventually lead back to California.

Elizabeth's odyssey through Hollywood brought her into contact with con men, pornographers, would-be

Elizabeth Short, the Black Dahlia

movie producers, hustlers, and crooks of all kinds. Along the way, she may have even had contact with a legitimate person now and then, but it seemed that she was destined to follow the route of exposure to the seamier side of life. During her stay in California, Elizabeth Short was transformed into the persona that became known as the Black Dahlia.

There have been various explanations about how she got the title. Although there may be disagreement about the actual source, it is clear that the title was based on the fact that Elizabeth dyed her hair black and was known to wear all black outfits of clothing. Possibly, she adopted the distinctive dark look in order to establish a single identity that would make her stand out in a crowd.

As the year 1946 drew to an end, Elizabeth Short, alias the Black Dahlia, found herself in financial trouble. She was without any steady place to live and found herself traveling from place to place in order to exist. On January 10, 1947, the Black Dahlia traveled from San Diego to Los Angeles with a traveling salesman. She checked her bag at a bus depot and hung around the Los Angeles Biltmore Hotel for an unknown reason. It was observed that she stayed near the lobby telephones and made at least one call and then waited for a call that apparently never came. At about 10:00 in the evening she left the hotel. The doorman tipped his hat to her as she walked away toward the unfortunate fate that would make her famous.

The exact events that brought about her death that followed her leaving the hotel remain open to speculation. After her body was found on January 15, 1947, the medical examiners estimated that she had died at around the midnight before the day her body was found. Could the Black Dahlia have gone off with her eventual killer right after she was seen leaving the hotel? What happened to the Black Dahlia for the several days between when she was last seen leaving the Biltmore Hotel and when her body was found? Was the Black Dahlia tortured by a mad killer who ended up mutilating her body, or was her death the result of contact with someone who was known to her from before? Some followers of the case have speculated that Elizabeth Short was the unfortunate victim of a tormentor who almost systematically tortured her for at least a couple of days while her wrists and ankles were bound with ropes. Her mutilated body showed the extent of the killer's deprivation. Could the killer have been motivated to perform the terrible acts against Elizabeth Short because of outrage against her, or was she a stranger to the killer?

Very little is really known about the personality of the killer. There has been a great deal of speculation as to what he or she may have been like. Ten days after Elizabeth Short's body was found, allegedly a box was found wrapped in plain brown paper. Next to it was a message made out from newspaper clippings that explained that the box contained belongings of the Black Dahlia and that a letter would follow. Inside were found the Black Dahlia's purse, birth certificate, social security card, various notes, personal papers, and address book. Someone, however, had ripped out a page of the address book. Did the killer purposely rip out the page of the address book to eliminate his own address and any other witnesses that might be able to direct the investigation toward him or her? No fingerprints or any other clues came out of the papers that would directly point at a killer. The police put a great many investigators on the street to interview scores of possible witnesses. The identity of the killer of the Black Dahlia remained unknown.

For many years after the killing, law enforcement officers continued to try to follow up the few clues that they had to the murder in order to reach a solution. Public interest in the macabre case of the killing of the Black Dahlia remained high. As is the case in many killings that are well publicized, thrill seekers and publicity hounds have tried to interject themselves into the case as witnesses or potential killers. Some versions of the legend of the Black Dahlia have made her appear as a bigger-than-life figure.

Unfortunately for Elizabeth Short, all of the notoriety came only after the tortured ending of her life. While she lived, she was not a starlet, but just another young person who had pursued the dream of fame and fortune in the movie capital to no avail. She did not live a glamorous existence, but experienced all the emotional turmoil and indignities that can come out of poverty. Just as the Black Dahlia figure was nothing but a fictional creation to begin with, so is the picture of Elizabeth Short as a glamorous Hollywood personality. The real Elizabeth Short was nothing but an emotionally tormented young person who tried to search out an identity for herself. Unfortunately, she was the poor victim of a sadistic killer who ended any possibility of her ever finding the happiness that her wandering spirit was intensely looking for in the shadowy fringes of the make-believe world of movie society.

8

John Dillinger

The early 1930s in America is often remembered for the daring criminals of the time that captured the imagination of the American public. Probably no one characterized the daring robber of the period more than John Dillinger. His career supposedly came to an end on the evening of July 22, 1934, in Chicago outside the Biograph Theater.

It seems that after Dillinger had earlier escaped from jail he eluded law enforcement officers throughout the country while still able to commit occasional crimes. He had the image of a "Robin Hood" to many, because he had a reputation for popularity among the common people while he robbed the wealthy. The fact that when he was involved in shooting matches with the police bystanders were injured was often neglected in relating his exploits. For example, when law enforcement officers in the city of St. Paul, Minnesota, tried to go after him, a shooting spree ensued. Dillinger managed to escape, but some innocent bystanders were shot. After the St. Paul incident supposedly a trap was set up for Dillinger in Chicago. An informer had told the police that Dillinger was living under the alias of Jimmy Lawrence. He had undergone plastic surgery to change his appearance and felt confident that he would not be recognized while operating under the alias of Jimmy Lawrence. On the evening Dillinger was allegedly shot and killed, he went to the movies with a young woman, Polly Hamilton, and Anna Stage, the famous woman in red. The older woman, Anna Stage, has been known by the outfit that she wore as the woman in red. The traditional story has been that she was a young and attractive beauty. Anna Stage, the former madam, had cooperated with the police in setting up Dillinger, alias Jimmy Lawrence, to be captured. It had been arranged that when the police, waiting outside the theater, saw Anna Stage in her red dress they would know that the man that was with her was John Dillinger. The officers watched Dillinger enter the theater with the two women and decided not to go after Dillinger immediately, because it might be dangerous to the public at that time. Instead, they waited until he left the theater. Later as Jimmy Lawrence, alias Dillinger, left the theater the agent in charge, Melvin Pervis, lit his cigar to signal other officers to move in and arrest the gangster. After Dillinger was asked to halt, he instead looked around and observed that the two women that he had been with had abandoned him. At this point, realizing his betrayal, he pulled his gun and ran into an alley. Law enforcement

John Dillinger

officers let loose with a hail of bullets. A person who was hit in the hail of bullets was Dillinger this time. One bullet supposedly passed right through his head.

Immediately after the shooting on July 22, 1934, there was great publicity for the fact that Dillinger's reign had ended. Yet, Dillinger, as with many famous people, was not easily killed off in the public mind. There have been questions as to whether the traditional story is correct for Dillinger's demise.

One theory is that the person who was really killed outside the Biograph Theatre was Jimmy Lawrence, a minor criminal who operated in Chicago. The comment has been made that once the law enforcement officers realized that they had killed the wrong man, either the police were really fooled or covered up the fact that they had killed the wrong man out of embarrassment. Nevertheless, the question comes up that if Jimmy Lawrence was really killed, then what evidence is there to support the fact that the man who was killed was not Dillinger?

In support of the theory that Dillinger was not the man who was shot, is the fact that the autopsy report seems to support this proposition. Supposedly the coroner's report cited that the Dillinger body had brown eyes, in spite of the fact that it has long been known that Dillinger had blue eyes. The dead man supposedly had a chronic heart condition. For those who follow the Dillinger exploits, it was believed that he was in excellent physical condition and that only someone in excellent physical condition could have performed the way he had. Besides, they reasoned, if he had a heart problem why wouldn't it have been detected at an earlier time when he joined the navy? Dillinger was known to be an avid baseball player and had never been known to have any limitations on his playing of sports such as baseball.

The size of the dead body seems to show that it was shorter and heavier than Dillinger was known to be. There even seems to be a question why the record of the dead body does not reflect the scar marks and wounds that Dillinger was thought to possess. There had even been a question of why the records do not clearly show that the dead body had shown no indication of plastic surgery to the face. It has been argued that the fingerprint card that allegedly showed that the dead man was Dillinger was planted in the morgue before the killing. Why, though, if law enforcement officers were initially fooled by the Jimmy Lawrence plan for Dillinger would they have earlier planted a card that showed Dillinger's fingerprints? Even if law enforcement officers did later find out that the wrong man was shot, would they or could they have successfully substituted a false card showing Dillinger's fingerprints? It has been argued that if Jimmy Lawrence was, in fact, the one killed instead of Dillinger, the question remains why no one who knew the real Lawrence ever came forward to state that he had, in fact, been killed rather than Dillinger. Possibly, more intriguing to the people who have followed the Dillinger legend was what really happened to Dillinger if he was not shot on that fateful evening in July of 1934.

One rumor has been that Dillinger, in fact, had plotted his own make-believe murder in order to allow him to escape the net that was coming down upon him by the law. After the shooting, it has been rumored that he moved out to the western part of the United States. The question still arises of how could someone like John Dillinger have continued to live quietly after the alleged murder without committing crimes? John Dillinger was known to be the type of restless spirit that always seemed to be on the go and loved the challenges involved in breaking the law. It is questionable that he could change his character so easily to be a law-abiding person.

Did Jimmy Lawrence originally agree to be a stand-in for Dillinger, or was he merely duped by the Dillinger gang into being at a spot where he would be killed? Did Dillinger know that he would be shot outside the Biograph Theater and purposely plan on putting another person in the position so that law enforcement officers would be fooled into believing that they had finally gotten their man? Even if Dillinger made such a plan, how did he know that the police would accept that he was, in fact, the person shot outside the theater after they examined the body? If the police did not plant the fingerprint card, then could John Dillinger himself arrange to have a false fingerprint card in place so that Jimmy Lawrence's body would be accepted as being that of Dillinger?

There are certainly many questions that have been raised by the facts surrounding Dillinger's alleged death. It is not, however, difficult to accept that in the carnival type of atmosphere that was in existence after it was announced that Dillinger had been killed, there may have been mistakes made in the preparation of autopsy papers. Perhaps in looking back, we may pay more attention to the importance of the paperwork than those who had to go through the procedure in 1934. Today there are those that argue that mistakes do happen periodically in coroner's offices and that it is possible that a few errors on paper mean that Dillinger was not killed outside the theater on July 22, 1934. Dillinger was a very difficult adversary to catch during the Depression Era and whether Dillinger was actually killed in 1934 or not, does not change the fact that the legend that he created has gone on. Possibly, the legendary Dillinger creates a far greater image than any single criminal could ever have hoped to have. Possibly the tremendous figure that was created has made it difficult for some people to accept his death. It is not unusual in the annals of history for a charismatic individual to be kept alive in the memories of those who took an interest in him.

If Dillinger was killed, the legend of his exploits will not so easily come to an abrupt end, but, in fact, may grow with time. This growing interest in him may explain why so many people have taken an interest in the theory that Dillinger survived the shooting outside the Biograph Theater on July 22, 1934.

Bibliography

Lizzie Borden

Aymar, Brandt and Edward Sagarin. *A Pictorial History of the World's Greatest Trials from Socrates to Jean Harris.* Bonanza Books, 1967 (p. 173).

Gustafson, Anita. *Guilty or Innocent?* New York: Holt, Rinehart, and Winston, 1985.

Lester, Henry. *Unsolved Murders and Mysteries.* Futura Books, 1987.

Martinez, Lionel. *Great Unsolved Mysteries of North America.* 1988 (p. 83).

Radin, Edward. *Lizzie Borden: The Untold Story.* New York: Simon and Schuster, 1961.

Spiering, Frank. *Lizzie.* New York: Pinnacle Books, 1984.

Sullivan, Robert. *Goodby Lizzie Borden.* Bhattleboro, VT: Stephen Greene Press, 1974.

Jack the Ripper

Begg, Paul. *Jack the Ripper: The Uncensored Facts.* Jersey City, NJ: Robson Books, 1988.

Evans, Stewart, and Paul Gainey. *Jack the Ripper—First American Serial Killer.* London: Arrow Books Ltd., 1995.

Harrison, Shirley, narr. *The Diary of Jack the Ripper: The Chilling Confessions of James Maybrick.* New York: Pocket Star Books, 1995.

Knight, Stephen. *Jack the Ripper: The Final Solution.* England: Treasure Press, 1976.

Noguchi, M.D., Thomas T., with Joseph Dimona. *Coroner at Large.* New York: Pocket Books, 1985.

Paley, Bruce. *Jack the Ripper: The Simple Truth.* London: Headline Book Publishing, 1996.

Rumbelow, Donald. *Jack the Ripper: The Complete Casebook.* New York: Contemporary Books, Inc., 1988.

Wilson, Colin, and Robin O'Dell. *Jack the Ripper.* London: Corgi Books, 1987.

Wilson, Colin. *Unsolved Classic True Murder Cases.* New York: Peter Bedrick Books, 1987 (p. 13).

Sir Harry Oaks

Bocca, Geoffrey. *The Life and Death of Sir Harry Oaks*. New York: Doubleday, 1959.

Jones, Richard Glyn. *Unsolved Classic True Murder Cases*. New York: Peter Bedrick Books, 1987 (p. 273).

Leasor, James. *Who Killed Sir Harry Oaks?* Boston: Houghton Mifflin Company, 1983.

Wilson, Kirk. *Unsolved Great Mysteries of the 20th Century*. New York: Carroll Graf Publishers, Inc., 1990 (p. 114).

Was Napoleon Bonaparte Murdered?

Brookes, Dame Mabel. *St. Helena Story*. New York: Dodd, Mead & Company, 1960.

Forshufvud, Sten. *Who Killed Napoleon?* Translated by Alan Houghton Brodrick. London: Hutchinson of London, 1961.

Gurney, Gene. *Kingdoms of Europe: An Illustrated Encyclopedia of Ruling Monarchs from Ancient Times to the Present*. New York: Crown Publishers, Inc., 1982 (p. 117).

Hardwick, Mollie. *Great Unsolved Mysteries*. Century Books, Ltd., 1984.

Maurois, André. *Napoleon: A Pictorial Directory*. New York: Viking Press, 1963.

Oronin, Vincent. *Napoleon Bonaparte: An Intimate Biography*. New York: William Morrow Company, Inc., 1971.

Weider, Ben, and David Hapgood. *The Murder of Napoleon*. New York: Congdon E. Lattes, Inc., 1982.

Dr. Sam Sheppard

Bailey, F. Lee, with Harvey Aronson. *The Defense Never Rests*. New York: Signet (from New American Library), 1971.

Gustafson, Anita. *Guilty or Innocent*. New York: Holt, Rinehart, and Winston, 1985.

Holmes, Paul. *The Sheppard Murder Case*. New York: David McKay Company, Inc., 1961.

Pollack, Jack Harrison. *Dr. Sam: An American Tragedy*. Chicago: Henry Regnery Company, 1972.

The Mysterious Death of William Taylor

Booth, Charles G., Mary Collins, Guy Endore, Erle Stanley Gardner, Geoffrey Homes, Eugene D. Williams, and George Worthing Yates. *Los Angeles Murders.* New York: Dvell, Sloan, and Pearce, 1947 (p. 85).

Graft, George C. *Celebrity Murders.* Pinnacle Books, Windsor Publishing Corp., 1990.

Kirkpatrick, Sidney D. *A Cast of Killers.* New York: Dutton, 1986.

Martinez, Lionel. *Great Unsolved Mysteries of North America.* (p. 93).

Munn, Michael. *The Hollywood Murder Casebook.* New York: St. Martin's Press, 1987.

Wolf, Marvin J., and Katherine Mader. *Fallen Angeles: Chronicles of L.A. Crime and Mystery.* New York: Ballantine Books, 1986.

The Black Dahlia

Martinez, Lionel. *Great Unsolved Mysteries of North America.* (p. 100).

Sifaki, Carl. *The Encyclopedia of American Crime.* New York: Facts on File, Inc., 1982.

Sterling, Hank. *Ten Perfect Crimes.* New York: Stravon Publishers, 1954 (p. 37).

Wolf, Marvin J., and Katherine Mader. *Fallen Angeles: Chronicles of L.A. Crime and Mystery.* New York: Ballantine Books, 1986.

John Dillinger

Nash, Jay Robert. *Almanac of World Crime.* New York: Bonanza Books, 1986.

Nash, Jay Robert. *Bloodletters & Badmen: A Narrative Encyclopedia of American Criminals from the Pilgrims to the Present.* New York: M. Evans and Company, Inc., 1973.

Nash, Jay Robert, and Ron Offen. *Dillinger: Dead or Alive?.* Chicago: Henry Regnery Company, 1970.

Scott, Sir Harold. *The Concise Encyclopedia of Crime and Criminals.* New York: Hawthorn Books, Inc., 1961.

Symons, Julian. *A Pictorial History of Crime.* New York: Bonanza Books, 1966.

Toland, John. *Dillinger Days.* New York: Random House, 1963.

About the Author

Fred Neff has had a life long interest in history and the law. From the time he was a young boy he has taken a special interest in studying true life criminal cases. As a part of his early interest in true crime mysteries Mr. Neff has made an extensive study of criminology, historical research methods and law enforcement investigation techniques.

Fred Neff graduated in 1970 from the University of Minnesota College of Education with High Distinction. He taught social studies in the Hopkins School system. He introduced the study of historical mysteries to his students to enhance their knowledge of the past and their problem-solving skills. The reception was so positive in his first year of teaching that the University of Minnesota assigned student teachers to Fred, so that they would be exposed to his teaching techniques. From 1972-1976 he attended William Mitchell College of Law. While attending law school he taught at the University of Minnesota, University of Wisconsin and Inver Hills College.

After graduating from law school in 1976 he served as a criminal prosecutor. Subsequently, he left public service as a prosecutor and was appointed to do criminal defense work for the Public Defenders Conflict Panel and Juvenile Justice Panel. He has also acted as private counsel on numerous criminal cases. As a part of his work as a lawyer he has dealt with extensive criminal investigations. Mr. Neff has taught classes for lawyers, legal personnel and law enforcement officers in handling criminal cases. He has also served as a legal advisor to peace officers and private investigators.

Mr. Neff's experience and knowledge in the field of legal matters has led to his election and appointment as a member of the board of directors of a number of organizations including a national insurance company. In 1989, Mr. Neff acted as a co-host on a television program Great Puzzles in History. Each program covered a different historical mystery. The show was very popular and ran continually from 1989-1991.

He has received many awards for his accomplishments and community involvement including the city of St. Paul Citizen of the Month Award in 1975, a Commendation for Distinguished Service from the Sibley County Attorney's office in 1980, the WCCO Good Neighbor Award in 1985, the HLS Justice Award in 1985, the Lamp of Knowledge award from the Twin Cities Lawyers Guild in 1986, commendation awards from N.W. Community T.V. 1989, 1990, and 1991, and the Presidential Medal of Merit Award from President George Bush in 1990.